W9-CHJ-794

ZEE EDGELL was born and grew up in Belize City, Belize. She is the author of *Beka Lamb* (Heinemann 1982), which was awarded the 1982 Fawcett Society Book Prize. She has also published *In Times Like These* (Heinemann 1991) and *The Festival of San Joaquin* (Heinemann 1997). One of her first jobs (in the early 1960s) was as a reporter on *The Daily Gleaner* in Kingston, Jamaica. From 1966 to 1968 she taught at St Catherine Academy and worked as the editor of a small newspaper in Belize City. She has lived in Jamaica, Britain, Afghanistan, Nigeria, Bangladesh and Somalia. In the early 1980s she returned to Belize to teach and served as the Director of the Women's Bureau in the Government of Belize (1981–82) and later as the Director of the Department of Women's Affairs (1986–87). She lectured at the University College of Belize from 1988 to 1989, and was a Visiting Writer in the Department of English at Old Dominion University, Norfolk, Virginia in the USA in 1993. Edgell's short story, 'My Uncle Theophilus', won the Canute A. Brodhurst Prize for short fiction and was published in *The Caribbean Writer* in 1999. She is currently an Associate Professor in the Department of English at Kent State University in Ohio, USA.

ZEE EDGELL

TIME AND THE RIVER

Heinemann

Heinemann Educational Publishers
Halley Court, Jordan Hill, Oxford OX2 8EJ
A part of Harcourt Education Limited

Heinemann: a member of the Reed Elsevier plc group.
361 Hanover Street, Portsmouth, NH 03801-3912, USA

OXFORD MELBOURNE AUCKLAND
JOHANNESBURG GABORONE KUALA LUMPUR
PORTSMOUTH (HN) USA CHICAGO

First published by Heinemann Educational Publishers in 2007

British Library Cataloguing in Publication Data
A catalogue record for this book is available from the British Library.

Library of Congress Cataloging in Publication Data

Edgell, Zee.
  Time and the river / Zee Edgell.
  p. cm. — (Caribbean writers series)
  ISBN-13: 978-0-435-21518-7
  ISBN-10: 0-435-21518-3
  1. Belize—Fiction. I. Title.
  PR9280.9.E34T56 2007
  813'.54—dc22

AFRICAN WRITERS SERIES and CARIBBEAN WRITERS SERIES and
their accompanying logos are trademarks in the United States of America
of Heinemann: a member of the Reed Elsevier plc group.

10 09 08 07
10 9 8 7 6 5 4 3 2 1

ISBN 0435 21518 3 / 978 0435 21518 7

Author photograph by Philip Stokes
Cover illustration by David Axtell
Design by Sara Rafferty

Acknowledgements

The lines from "Diving into the Wreck". Copyright © 2002 by Adrienne Rich.
Copyright © 1973 by W. W. Norton & Company, Inc, from THE FACT OF A
DOORFRAME: SELECTED POEMS 1950-2001 by Adrienne Rich. Used by
permission of the author and W. W. Norton & Company, Inc.

Printed and bound in England by Ashford Colour Press

To my family

I came to explore the wreck.
The words are purposes.
The words are maps.
I came to see the damage that was done
and the treasures that prevail.
I stroke the beam of my lamp
slowly along the flank
of something more permanent
than fish or weed

the thing I came for:
the wreck and not the story of the wreck
the thing itself and not the myth
the drowned face always staring
toward the sun
the evidence of damage
worn by salt and sway into this threadbare beauty
the ribs of the disaster
curving their assertion
among the tentative haunters.

From 'Diving into the Wreck' by Adrienne Rich (1973)

Chapter 1

THE BAY OF HONDURAS
UPRIVER, MAY 1798
LEAH

Leah Lawson sat beside her friend Will McGilvrey on the ground at the back of a thatched hut in the shade of mango and cashew trees. Their eyes were fixed on the family of deaf-mutes who had emerged without warning, as they usually did, from the thick bush and the nearly impenetrable forests which surrounded the clearing.

'I feel a bit strange when I see them nowadays, especially the man with the limp,' Leah said. She held the wooden bucket against her chest, feeling the coolness of the wet staves through the worn fabric of her grey linen smock.

For most of the morning, Leah had been filling with well-water the six barrels ranged along an outside wall of the hut which served as the cookhouse. She was now waiting until the father, mother and two sons had traversed the path that led past the well, the wash-tubs and makeshift sheds to a wider footpath through the bush to the river. Most of the smaller huts were empty now and for a second year they had not been repaired or made ready for a new season.

'Strange, how?' Will asked, getting up and walking across the clearing. He selected a large calabash from a number of gourds hanging on pegs inserted in a post of the hut. Will dipped it into a barrel, scooping out water and splashing it over his face, shoulders and arms. In the pause they heard coconut oil sputtering in a pan on the indoor fire-hearth. Leah's mother, Hannah, was frying slices of a sergeant fish which Will had caught near the mangrove swamps, on his way to Lawson's Camp.

Leah shrugged but did not reply. Her gaze lingered for a moment on the younger of the two sons, who walked more slowly than the others, as though the sole of his left foot was injured. Like the rest of his family, he had shiny yellow hair, except that his had been cropped close to his skull. 'Perhaps he's had lice,' Leah thought, for when she'd last seen him his hair had been shoulder-length. His pale blue eyes were watchful as though he was fearful of a surprise attack. 'As well he might be,' Leah thought to herself, putting a hand on her throat, which had tightened. She swallowed but her mouth was dry. 'I'm frightened too,' she thought, 'mostly of everyone and everything nowadays.'

Will wiped his face, neck and arms on a piece of cotton, faded and threadbare. He gave Leah a shrewd, sidelong glance before folding the cloth carefully and sticking it into his waistband. 'Don't worry about them. They don't own much, 'cept their own selves.'

'Which is more than we do,' Leah said. Will knew a lot about scouting for fresh stands of mahogany but she wasn't sure he knew all that much about her life in the camp. He worked at a mahogany bank, some distance away near Roaring Creek; Leah had never been there. She couldn't remember seeing his master, Thomas McGilvrey, in Belize Town and Will seldom spoke his name or talked very much about his experiences at Roaring Creek.

'You're too 'fraida, that's your trouble,' Will said. 'Good thing I'm around to look out for you.' He glanced at her again, smiling. 'Anyway, most likely they won't be back here.'

'How do you know?' Leah asked, listening to the rustling of the dried leaves, red, gold and brown, which covered the path. The deaf-mutes carried bundles of food and clothing, a few cooking utensils, muskets, machetes and axes, the usual things people carried when travelling for any distance through the bush.

Will shrugged, resuming his scrutiny of the family as they neared a bend in the path near the huts. 'More fighting. Soldiers on the way, people say.' He spat a stream of tobacco juice to a spot a yard or so from where he sat.

'Disgusting,' Leah said but Will only laughed. He'd been chewing tobacco regularly since he'd started his new job a few months before; when he'd been sent into the bush to help the men who were skilled in locating mahogany trees. The merchants said mahogany was beginning to be profitable overseas.

'Stops me thinking about food,' Will said. 'No cooking fires in the bush at any time now.' He sniffed the air appreciatively. 'Fish smells good,' he said.

'Are you and Sharper in the fighting against Mr Lawson, Mr McGilvrey and the other masters?' Leah liked Sharper, a short, stocky man with bright brown eyes and a deep voice.

'Who told you that?' Will asked, unrolling a sailcloth bag in which he would pack the day's meal to share with Sharper and their other friends.

'Nobody told me anything. Are you, Will?' Leah noted the pouches beneath his eyes, large and dark.

'What do you think?' he asked, one eyebrow raised.

'I think you are. You act different.'

'How so?' Will asked.

'Secretive – like you are hiding something.'

He smiled, then sucked his teeth as though dismissing her fears. 'Think all you want. Just keep quiet about it.'

In a few weeks the slave revolt would surely be over one way or another. Will would then probably go back to helping Dover, the chief mahogany huntsman at McGilvrey Bank, to cut through the most inaccessible parts of the forest to the highest spot of ground they could find. Will would climb the very tallest tree he could see. Sometimes he'd stand on high hills of limestone blocks and rubble scattered in various parts of the bush. People believed that these ruins, covered by bushes and trees, were temples used by the Maya Indians a long time ago. On a sunny day from the top of the tree, or from one of these Maya temples, the forest would spread out before him like a grass-green sea for miles in every direction. Will had told Leah he didn't really mind climbing up so high because then he was alone, in charge of himself, at least for a little while.

In August and September, the leaves of the mahogany tree turned a yellowish or reddish hue. Sometimes if he saw a spot in the bush where the mahogany trees seemed plentiful, Will would descend and lead Dover and the other men, without a compass or other guide, to the area where the trees were located. Each tree was carefully marked and the bush cleared, creating trails which led from one tree to the next.

Dover was growing old and soon he would be forced to relinquish his position as the head huntsman; his damaged knees made walking and climbing a difficult and painful job. Although Will had never said so, Leah knew Will wanted Dover's job, which was a prestigious one in the settlement. Ordinary slaves, like herself, were usually sold for around a hundred and thirty Jamaican pounds but a huntsman like Dover was worth as much as five hundred British pounds, or so she'd heard. Huntsmen were treated well, for the owner of a good mahogany huntsman would not want him to reveal where new stands of mahogany had been seen and secretly lead a more generous paymaster to the spot. The British settlers' wealth was in slaves because Spain's claim to the entire area did not permit the British to own land, establish estates or build fortifications.

She glanced at Will, whose gaze still lingered on the youngest deaf-mute. Like his father and brother, he wore a dark shirt, braces and loose, black trousers that were patched in several places.

Will fiddled with the waistband of his short trousers, held up by a rope made from the tit-tie vine. 'No danger 'bout here,' he said, 'I keep a lookout for you and Hannah.'

'But you're not always here,' Leah said, realizing that her increasing anxiety somehow had to be overcome, or at least disguised until she felt stronger, but she had no clear idea how this might be done.

She looked behind her to the doorway of the hut in which she slept with her mother and Samuel, her younger brother. The walls of the hut were made of palmetto poles and thatched with dried leaves from the cohune palm. Inside were Will's musket, machete and axe. She thought about the terrifying nightly events and wondered about Will's part in them. He was several years older than she was. They had sometimes tried by various calculations to guess by how much but they remained uncertain about the number of years between their ages.

'I was about your age now,' Will had said, 'when the Jamaican ship first brought me here.' Will seldom talked to Leah about his life in Africa, or his journey from there, but Leah knew it was often on his mind.

'When was that?' Leah asked, thinking about Will's accent which sounded so different from the way people spoke who had been born in the settlement.

'About ten, fifteen years ago, maybe. There were slave risings then too, so I remember.'

She tried to imagine a much younger Will slipping barefoot along the green aisles of the bush in this new country. He would have been on the constant lookout for snakes, pumas, ocelots or anything else he thought could possibly harm him if he relaxed his vigilance. In her mind, she saw him paddling a dorey along the rivers, creeks and lagoons, or submerging himself in the river with only his eyes and nose above the waterline.

'I'm only afraid sometimes at night, Will,' she said. There were so many strange, often frightening things happening in other camps up and down the river that Leah and her family didn't go there to bathe anymore. She'd once seen a tommy-goff snake wriggling beside her in the river, and had dashed out of the water, squelching up the muddy riverside to slightly higher ground. Since then, Leah had bathed only near the edges of the river, keeping a sharp lookout all the while for river snakes and alligators. Thick bushes and enormous trees threw grotesque shadows on the water there.

Once she'd mistaken a stump of wood projecting above the surface of the river for an alligator, which was really a crocodile, or so she'd heard people say. Sometimes it was hard for Leah to know what to believe. She gave a slight shudder. Tommy-goffs, crocodiles or alligators were the least of her worries now. 'Everything around here gives me goose bumps nowadays,' she said.

'Me too,' Will said, 'most of the time.' He stretched out on the ground, propping himself up on his elbows. He gazed at a narrow strip of blue sky visible through the lower branches of the mango trees towering above the makeshift huts in the clearing. 'Backabush we see tigers, snakes, mountain cows and all that. You'll get used to it.'

'Doesn't sound to me like you've gotten used to it,' Leah said. 'Besides there are no tigers back there – jaguars, maybe.' She was glad to say this since she felt Will was nearly always right in his knowledge about the bush and often discounted her fears because she'd been born and brought up in Belize Town.

'Go away with you, Leah,' he said. 'Every soul 'round here calls them tigers. They must know.'

'You ever see one?' She really wanted to hear more about the revolt, about who was winning and who was losing, and so she was sorry they had gotten into one of their silly arguments.

'One of what?' He yawned.

'Those so-called tigers then.'

'Plenty,' Will said, putting a plug of tobacco into his mouth.

Leah sighed. He was offended now and probably glad for an excuse not to tell her anything more about the fighting which she feared was coming nearer to Lawson's camp.

Chapter 2

They were both quiet for a while, watching the family of deaf-mutes as they slipped into the bush on the far side of the clearing. The clearing was similar to so many others up and down the river. Each mahogany 'bank', or 'work', had its encampments with huts and small cultivations called 'plantations' where plantains, yams, sweet potatoes and a variety of other ground food and vegetables usually grew in abundance. But these everyday sources of food were greatly depleted as almost every kind of work in the forests and in the clearings was at a standstill.

Leah looked at Will, who was lying flat on the ground now, using his hands and arms as a pillow under his head. Through the leaves of the mango trees, the sun flickered onto his face. He closed his eyes and after a while his even breathing told her he was fast asleep. Perhaps he felt safe sleeping beside her and for a moment she wondered about this. Then her thoughts returned to the family slowly making their way to the riverside where they would wait for a large dorey or pit-pan willing and able to take them as passengers.

Will had said they were probably gone for good and perhaps he was right. Nobody seemed to know or care very much about them and they never seemed to have any visitors to their house, which was little more than an isolated shack in the bush.

People always referred to them as deaf-mutes but Leah could never quite understand what that meant. How could it be that nobody in the family could speak or hear?

It was a sad thing for her to contemplate. She decided she'd try to find out one of these days, maybe when the fighting was over, although it was difficult for her to imagine what her life would be like then. 'Probably just as it is now,' Leah thought to herself. She was surprised to discover that she was hoping that the uprising in the forests, on the rivers and on the creeks would somehow make things at least a little better in all their lives.

She thought of the youngest son, the one with the limp, and of the funny sounds he made with his mouth. At first he had tried to make friends with her, at least she thought that was what he'd been doing. He'd offered her mangoes and cashews as if mangoes, cashews and other fruits weren't common on the ground all around the huts and everywhere else for miles. His actions puzzled then frightened her, for he always seemed to appear when few people were in the clearing, which was very often now, since the uprising began.

He would emerge smiling and without a sound on the path in front of her, his head tilted to one side and his big hands filled with fruit. He had a narrow face, large ears and eyes that changed from blue to grey in the light flickering through the leaves. The second time he'd surprised her she'd run back to the main hut through the layers of fallen leaves, ankle deep on the ground, their crackling sound loud in her ears like approaching rain on faraway trees. Dozens of mangoes lay rotting in heaps on the path. She hated the squishy, sticky feeling of over-ripe fruit squelching between her toes and the buzzing flies and other insects crawling along her face, arms and legs. After the boy had gone, she'd waited until there were a few older men outside the huts sharpening machetes or feeding the oxen used for hauling the mahogany logs to the river. Then she'd rushed back to the well, its opening surrounded by wide wooden planks on the ground. She'd picked up her bucket and, standing a few feet away from the edge, flung it over the sides.

It splashed into the greenish water so far down in the earth. People said the well was older than any living person and it was easy to believe. Nobody really knew what was down there rotting in its depths: animals perhaps, birds and other things like fallen leaves and fruit of various kinds. She'd pulled on the rope, hauling up the bucket, eager to feel the cool water splashing over her feet. It removed the sticky dust and the bits of hairy fruit clinging to her toes.

Leah smelt the ripened cashews that had fallen to the ground. They were fermenting and a strong scent like wine was carried on the breeze from the corner of the clearing where numerous cashew trees grew. In the cool of the evening she would perform one of her other tasks, gathering the ripened fruit for stewing in sugar. But now, she reminded herself, there was probably not even enough sugar for tea. The arrival of doreys and pit-pans, loaded down with supplies from town, had been the high point of the month but for the past few weeks boats, empty or full, were rarely seen on the river.

Still, she could screw the grey nuts out of the flesh of the yellow, juicy, cashew fruit and set them out to dry. Later, when life was back to normal, she'd have them ready for roasting in the ashes of a bonfire of leaves and sticks. When the outside shells of the nuts were burnt to charcoal black and after they had cooled, she would break them open with a stone and remove the kernels. They always fetched a good price from the boatmen who sold them at the market in town.

Would things ever be quite the same again? She glanced at Will's long legs straight out before him. His feet, like her own, were bare. She listened to the rustling leaves of the common mango trees. These large mangoes were her favourite because their greenish-yellow skins peeled back neatly from the butter-yellow flesh which was never too sweet or too sour but something in between. In season they provided her with satisfying meals which helped to ease the hunger pains that gnawed constantly at her stomach.

She knew that it was not only a hunger for food that she tried to satisfy in the season of mangoes and cashews. It was also a hunger for freedom which everyone, she believed, wanted with a passion and which they took whenever the opportunity presented itself. Some people fled through miles of bush, trying to cross the borders away from the British settlement to the Spanish territories. It was said that the settlers there gave runaway slaves their freedom, asking only that they be baptized in the Roman Catholic faith. Many perished during these dangerous treks through the forests.

Leah did not yet want to go anywhere, except back to Belize Town, where she'd often seen the kind of life she hoped to have one day. She thought of the Clare sisters, independent and free. They did fine needlework for the wealthy in a small house overlooking Haulover Creek which emptied into the Caribbean Sea.

It was Miss Roslyn Clare who had put the idea of going to see Graham Lawson, Leah's father, into her head. One Saturday morning she'd said, 'He might allow you, Hannah and Sam to use the empty huts in the compound. He's had to sell a few people.' She unhooked the white cotton curtains from a parlour window and placed them on the pile of laundry in Leah's arms.

'Do you really think so, Miss Roslyn?' Leah asked, looking at the dubious frown on Miss Roslyn's face.

'Maybe not,' Miss Roslyn said, not meeting Leah's eyes. 'He's one of the harder cases. We need to pray for him.'

In the end Miss Roslyn and Leah decided to abandon the whole idea. They both had a strong feeling that Graham Lawson was likely to regard such a request as unnecessary provocation, insolence or insubordination. The laws and customs in the settlement often seemed arbitrary and unjust to Leah. She did not always understand them as well as the Clare sisters did.

Graham Lawson was a Scottish mahogany trader and slave owner, who had fathered several children in the settlement. The only other one of his children that Leah really knew was Sukie, who worked for Master Preston Dickey, the apothecary, and his Creole mistress, Orissa Caslow. People said Orissa Caslow practised obeah and had great power in the settlement.

'Mistress is a suspicious-minded woman,' Sukie had said. 'She thinks everybody is a thief. She counts every handkerchief, every fippence, two times over when I get in at night. Do I look like a thief to you? Just tell me straight.' She'd held her arms akimbo, frowning ferociously at Leah.

'No, you don't,' Leah said, thinking of Sukie's great interest in the apothecary's shop, with its tiny drawers crammed with powders and pills. She'd hate to lose her place there, where she was learning so much about the art of healing.

Short and stout, Sukie had usually been friendly on the few occasions when they'd met in the market, where Sukie peddled silk handkerchiefs from a tray hung by a fraying cloth around her neck. Leah decided that if ever she had another opportunity, she'd try to be better friends with Sukie. However, friendship with Sukie might not be easy as she never missed the chance to let people know that her mother, now deceased, had been an Indian from the Miskito Shore. It was Sukie's misfortune, she said, to be held illegally as a slave in the settlement.

'British law says that Miskito Indians are not to be slaves but here I am,' Sukie said, folding and unfolding the imported handkerchiefs on her wide wooden tray.

It was almost the only topic of conversation between them whenever they met. Leah smiled, thinking of the indignation which flashed in Sukie's dark eyes as she spoke about the injustice of their situation, which was as much an obsession for Sukie as it was for Leah.

Chapter 3

Leah had long known who her father was and he knew her but they had never acknowledged any family connection in public. Sometimes, if he met her emerging from an alleyway with a bundle of laundry on her head or hurrying along a back street in Belize Town, he bowed his head slightly or lightly touched the brim of his black hat. More often than not, however, he kept his eyes averted, pretending that he was unaware of her presence on the narrow streets of the small town.

She accepted his actions as only right and proper in their respective situations. Until her family had been summarily sent upriver, she had rarely felt anything more than the vaguest resentment or hurt whenever she saw her father from a distance. Leah often saw him entering the Court House to attend a magistrates' meeting, or standing at the creek-side talking with other mahogany merchants. Leah did not really expect any favours or consideration from her father. In this respect, he was similar to the reputed fathers of many slaves and free people of colour she knew in their settlement by the sea.

Saturdays were supposed to be free days for the slaves in the settlement. This enabled Leah to do the laundry for the Clare sisters in exchange for them teaching her to read, sew and embroider. Graham Lawson had never interfered with this arrangement, for which Leah had always been grateful.

Now she felt angry and upset that Ma Hannah, who was ill, and Samuel, only nine years old, had been brought upriver, against the usual custom. They were to work for Daniel Sproate, Lawson's white agent, and the male slaves remaining in Graham Lawson's mahogany camp. Many of Lawson's other slaves were hiding out in caves or in places like Runaway Creek. Some were trying to make their way to the Spanish border.

Trying not to think about this, Leah gave a loud sigh. She

was about to rise to her feet and pick up her buckets when Will reached across and put one arm over her shoulder. This made her uncomfortable so she removed it.

'Leah,' he said, 'let's you and me be sweethearts.' He touched the scars on his face, moving his fingers back and forth as though he was trying to memorize the pattern.

'I thought you were asleep,' she said, trying to smile naturally. She didn't want to hurt Will – he was her friend. Still, her heart was beating rapidly and she was sure her discomfort showed on her face.

'How about it?' Will asked.

'Hand me those buckets!' she said, as he began swinging them in his hand, out of her reach. 'I am never going to be anyone's sweetheart.'

'Yes you will Leah, and one day you'll be glad to have me.' His voice was full of warmth and he still smiled at her with great fondness.

'Did someone tell you that?' Leah asked. She felt a growing ache in her stomach and she could feel her lips beginning to tremble. Will was becoming more important with every day the fighting lasted. She looked into his eyes, large and dark, with long lashes. People said his eyesight was so keen he could spot mahogany trees miles away in the bush. If Will were to ask for her, Graham Lawson, his white son or their agents would probably agree. So might Thomas McGilvrey, who was Graham Lawson's business associate, perhaps even his friend for all Leah knew. 'Why do you say that, Will?'

'I like you and I feel sorry for you as well sometimes.' He looked down at the buckets he held in one hand before setting them down near her feet. 'I know you like me.'

'Yes, but I don't want to have a sweetheart,' Leah said. She picked up the buckets, glad to have something to do with her hands, glad that her heart wasn't beating so fast any more. 'I want...

I want...'

'What?' He was still smiling but his eyes had narrowed to almost a squint. Then his face grew suspicious.

'Oh, I don't really know Will, I don't.' She didn't want to lie, but she couldn't bring herself to tell him that she already loved someone else. She had glimpsed another life, one that in her dreams already belonged to her. During the past year, those dreams had transported her out of the squalor and misery of her days and the more recent terror of her nights.

She seemed to have loved Josiah for as long as she had known him. They'd become good friends during the years she had helped with the laundry at his home on the Foreshore. He had taught her many useful things and lent her books which she mostly kept at the home of the Clare sisters. They advised her not to let others know she was learning to read.

'If Josiah's parents find out, who knows where that would lead?' Miss Roslyn had said.

His family had never discovered that Josiah allowed her to choose books from the shelves in his bedroom at the top of the house. The Potts' three-storeyed house was so high that, standing at one of the four windows, Leah could see the wide creek flowing into the sea and almost the entire town. While the family was at lunch or tea, she often walked along the verandahs outside Josiah's bedroom. Sometimes she climbed to the lookout room which had a small verandah, jutting out from the rooftop. The room contained instruments for looking out to sea and for examining the sky at night.

She had once been taken by the Potts family to St George's Caye on their holiday to help with the water-carrying and the laundry. That had been a grand April, the best time she'd ever had. The caye had been the first capital in the settlement. The settlers also kept spare stores and arms on the caye. People went there for honeymoons or when they were ill and needed to recuperate.

She'd envied those slaves who lived almost permanently on the caye. Many of them worked for fisherfolk, turtlers or as domestics. The island had seemed idyllic to her and the lives of the slaves seemed freer, less brutal. What impressed her there was the silence, except for the sound of the waves mingling with the wind rustling the coconut palms. She ate large quantities of the coco-plums which grew wild. In the evenings Leah walked in the cemetery trying to decipher the names and dates on the crumbling gravestones. The smell of salted fish, strung out to dry on the piers, permeated the air. She'd felt healthier too. The white sand was clean, cool and soothing between her toes. Morning and evening bathing in the sea were only a few steps away.

There was no shortage of food on the island and she had only to go to Fisherman's Town to obtain fish for her evening meal. Sometimes the men scaled and gutted the fish for her, throwing the innards over the sides of their boats for the seagulls and pelicans which swooped down to scoop up the discarded entrails. In the evening she went to the cookhouse where she was allowed to fry her fish or grill it on the beach with wood from the storehouse.

The Potts family was wealthy and they associated with church members, the magistrates and other prominent people. They entertained important visitors to the settlement, including the Spanish officials who descended on the town every now and then to make sure the settlers were not violating any treaties by building fortifications or establishing large plantations.

Leah admired Josiah very much. He never made her feel like a slave and he'd been kind to her from the time they'd first met in his parents' yard, while she was helping to hang laundry on the lines. In those days he'd still liked to play marbles, fly kites and practise spinning his top with his friends.

She'd listened closely to Josiah's speech, trying to speak like he did in clear, persuasive tones. Many of the slaves who occupied the rooms in the yard where Leah lived spoke harshly to each other, chiefly from necessity. Most of them were exhausted for much of the time. They were hungry, ill or desperate to say what had to be said in order to gain time in which to savour a bit of peace and quiet.

Leah glanced up at Will, who looked down at her expectantly. To her he was a reliable friend in a crowd of shifting people who were mostly strangers.

'I don't know, Will,' she said again. Only she did know. But how could she tell him that what she wanted most in the world was to be independent and free like the Clare sisters?

Will now looked miserable, as though he hadn't expected her to reply as she did. The expression on his face told her that he was now half inclined to disbelieve her.

So she said, 'I don't know why, Will, but if ever I own a mahogany works – I never will, of course – but if ever I do, you'll be captain of my works.'

Will laughed. His handsome face seemed to light up inside and he rubbed the side of his huge nose. He entered the hut and emerged with his musket, axe and machete which he slid into the worn leather sheath before buckling the belt around his waist.

'Bargain, Will?' Leah asked, fearful that he would refuse, that he would become annoyed, even angry with her.

'Bargain then, Leah,' he said. 'That's all right for now anyway.' He rubbed a finger up and down her right cheek then, whistling softly, he walked rapidly away across the clearing.

'He must have been joking,' Leah said to herself as she made her way slowly towards the well at the end of the clearing. 'I am sure he didn't mean it.' What had possessed her to tell Will that one day she hoped to own a mahogany camp and one large enough to need a captain? The whole idea seemed so ludicrous when she'd said it aloud, although she'd often heard of former slave men and women who now owned slaves and were holders of wood-cutting claims along the many rivers and creeks.

The day had grown more humid. Sweat poured down her face. Yet she felt chilled inside, somewhere near her heart, which was beating now too rapidly for comfort. As she hauled up a second bucket of water, a new fear struck her so forcibly that the rope, slimy and wet, slipped from her hands and the bucket fell back into the well. Just suppose Will, in his joking way, decided to tell her mother, or other people, what she'd said!

By now he was probably paddling a dorey across the river on his way back to the McGilvrey camp, or to one of the many caves where runaway slaves sometimes hid. He would probably tell Sharper what she'd said and what a laugh they'd have about that. Leah was relieved she hadn't told Will that what she wanted most was rarely possible in the settlement. She wanted a legal marriage, a family and a home. Marriage was actively discouraged, in the harshest ways, amongst people like Will and herself.

Chapter 4

Leah tried to put Will's proposal out of her mind as she carried buckets of water from the well to the barrels, emptied them and returned to the well. She thought of Josiah, whose occasional Saturday evening visits to the Clares' house had, for an hour or so, made such a difference to her week.

'I'll give you a hand with that,' the elder Miss Clare had said the last Saturday Leah had been in their home – several weeks before. Miss Roslyn had taken one end of a cotton sheet and helped Leah to fold it into a neat square. Freshly laundered towels, sheets and pillowcases were piled in the middle of the mahogany four-poster bed with its slender, graceful uprights. Over several months Leah had gradually reached the conclusion from one or two remarks made by the sisters that the bed had been a gift from a benefactor. She had never asked about the reason for such a generous gift although she longed to know.

The Clare sisters' reticence about their private affairs did not surprise Leah, for it was difficult to know whom to trust. Confidences were only shared after a long acquaintance. Leah had grown to womanhood knowing that the settlement was often an unpredictable, dangerous place where betrayals were common, revenge was swift (and even deadly) and misfortune was a part of everyday life.

'Leah, this is a hard thing for me to say but Josiah won't be allowed to visit us any more,' Miss Roslyn Clare said, moving from the bed to the wall cupboards, carrying armfuls of folded laundry ready for another day when Leah would press them with a flat-iron.

She had never suffered from seasickness but now Leah imagined that the queer sensation rising in her stomach, like a swift current running through her insides, was probably what it felt like. Saliva, tasting unpleasantly salty then sour, gathered at the

26

back of her throat, flooding her mouth.

'Has Josiah done something wrong, Miss Roslyn?' Leah asked, carefully smoothing out an embroidered pillowcase. Her fingers lingered on the raised knots in the centre of a beautiful red rose. Miss Roslyn and her sister Miss Evelyn were well known in the settlement for their fine handwork and for sewing. For a long time Leah had been learning all they were willing to teach her. She dreamed of the day when she would be able to set herself up as they had done.

Miss Roslyn Clare did not reply immediately. She bundled up another sheet in her short, plump arms and walked over to a rocking chair that was shaped like an enormous barrel. The chair had been put very close to a window overlooking the street, now muddy after the previous night's rain. She peered through the wooden louvres weathered to a grey the colour of ashes. The slats rattled softly in the March breeze.

Miss Roslyn sat there in a dark green dress, smoothing out the wrinkles in the sheet with her strong fingers. The sunlight from the window seemed to deepen the lines on her light brown skin, which reminded Leah of the caramel she'd seen her mother make in the houses where she had worked.

Miss Roslyn fingered a large, black mole which protruded from the right corner of her upper lip. She often did this when she was thinking things through. 'The two of you haven't done anything wrong here, Leah, but you know how people talk in this town.'

'About Josiah visiting you when I am here?' Leah asked, thinking of the occasions when, after his visit to the Clares was over, he'd wait for her outside the gate.

'Now, Leah,' Miss Roslyn said, 'you know that it is more than that nowadays. Evelyn and I can see your feelings. I wish that things were different but we can't afford accusations from Josiah's parents. I am counting on you to be sensible, Leah.'

'Don't you like Josiah any more, Miss Roslyn?' Leah asked, thinking of the Saturday before when she had sat with Josiah on the banks of the creek. His arms were around her shoulders as they'd looked out at the winking lights of the ships at anchor far out in the moonlit bay.

'Of course I like Josiah but Evelyn and I need to think about our little sewing business and about you. We wouldn't mind if anything good could come of it.'

As she talked, trying to explain in her gentle voice, Leah continued to stack the folded laundry at the foot of the bed in which both sisters slept, canopied by voluminous mosquito netting. The bed occupied most of the space in the front bedroom. There was a smaller bedroom to the rear of the house where the sisters kept their order books, papers, old trunks filled with threads, imported cloth, wool, needles and other supplies. But each sister had coveted the mahogany four poster bed in the front bedroom with its view of the road and creek, where they could see sailing boats, pit-pans and mahogany logs lashed together to form rafts.

Leah could feel Miss Roslyn's eyes on her back as she stood on tiptoe to place the sheets on the highest shelf. She felt thankful that her small, narrow feet were not only clean but carefully oiled. Leah enjoyed the feel of the polished pinewood floor beneath her bare feet. The bright blue colour of her frock, made from a coarse linen fabric, had been washed away but it was clean and neatly pressed. She had hoped that Josiah would visit that day but that was out of the question now. Her throat ached and her eyes filled with tears.

On that last Saturday night she had allowed Josiah to draw her close to rest her head on his shoulder and to return his kisses. His strong shoulders had felt like the safest harbour in her life.

'We'll get married,' he'd said, 'just as soon as we can raise the money to gain your freedom.' He'd raised her head, looked into her eyes and said, 'I love you so much.'

'I love you Josiah,' she'd replied, breathing in the scent of the sea mixed with the sweetness of Josiah's breath.

Miss Roslyn rose from the chair, which continued to rock gently back and forth. 'So you mustn't put your heart on seeing him here this afternoon,' she said, 'I told Evelyn to warn him off.'

'Warn who off, sister?' Miss Evelyn Clare, tall and slender, stood in the doorway wearing a bright pink dress trimmed with white. She held a cloth bundle of powder buns she had brought in from the kitchen. As a precaution against fire, the kitchen was built several yards from the main house.

'Josiah, who else? I was explaining why we can't encourage him to come here anymore. We'll all miss our evenings. He is such a good reader, the way he changes voices for every character in *Robinson Crusoe* is like a miracle.'

'He'd make a good actor,' Miss Evelyn said. 'In any case, I decided against telling him anything. It's his parents' place to tell him what's what.' She placed the bundle on top of the chest of drawers above which was a large oval mirror. There would be no setting of the table today, no boiling of water for tea with Josiah, no watching at the window for his arrival, no reading of the next chapter.

Miss Evelyn crossed the room and picked up the ruffles for a yellow skirt she was hand stitching. 'I expect they've told him already,' she said, tapping her middle finger, encased in a silver thimble, on the arm of the barrel-shaped rocking chair.

The sound made Leah's heart beat faster. 'Excuse me Miss Roslyn, Miss Evelyn, I'll be going now unless you need me to do something else.'

They both looked at Leah, their kind faces full of embarrassment and sadness, which made the tears roll down her face.

'Don't cry so, Leah. We know how you feel but it is all for the best,' Miss Roslyn said, giving Leah a hug as they walked to the back door. 'We'll see you next week, all right? Take care of yourself now.'

'Yes, Miss Clare, you do the same,' Leah said, slipping through the open door.

Outside the house she put on her boots, lifted her skirt and walked through the muddy yard until she reached the side of the road. She looked towards the creek but Josiah wasn't waiting for her that afternoon. Her belief in Josiah was so strong, however, that it wasn't long before the memory of his avowal of love and the plans they had made filled her heart and mind. How surprised and happy for her the Clare sisters would be when she was able to tell them all about it. The Clare sisters were the nicest people she knew.

That afternoon, when she arrived at the room she shared with her mother and Sam, she found them packing up their few belongings in two straw baskets. Her mother told her that the following morning they would be sent, with several other people, upriver to the Lawson mahogany camp. Hannah had been told that it was only a temporary measure, for their own good, as food was becoming scarce in town. Leah knew that this was only a partial truth. Leah wondered whether Graham Lawson had received word from Josiah's parents that she would no longer be employed in their home. It was unlikely, Leah knew, that she would ever learn the truth from anyone but Josiah.

Upriver Hannah, Leah and Sam had begun planting small provision grounds for the camp. Near the end of their first few weeks, Leah had heard from her mother that a few white men had been killed in several settlements which had been taken over by slaves who had risen up against their owners. It was difficult for Leah to know what to believe but the past few days had showed her how much worse their lives could become.

The sun was setting by the time Leah had finished filling the barrels. She stared down at her shadowed reflection in the cask of water near the spot where she and Will had sat earlier in the day, observing the deaf-mutes walking across the clearing to the path leading to the river. If she and her family managed to survive this latest conflict, she would try to return to Belize Town at the first opportunity. She needed to see Josiah, to hear his reassurances, to renew her belief in his love and her faith in his promises.

Chapter 5

There was a great commotion outside the huts in the clearing. The noise woke Leah. She sat up quickly, her heart thumping loudly, wondering who had been wounded now, or even killed. For a few moments she felt unable to move. She had been dreaming that she was lashed to an enormous raft of mahogany logs which was hurtling along the river in flood. In the dream, the water rolled over her. She felt unable to breathe or move her arms and legs. The rushing water filled her lungs as she was forced to inhale.

Leah sat on the edge of the wooden cot, hugging her knees, willing herself to forget the nightmare. She needed to be calm, to think, to make sure she was able to survive the ongoing fight in the bush and on the rivers and creeks. She peered through the gloom to where Samuel slept on another bunk in the corner of the hut. He was still there and safe but her mother was gone and she could tell that daylight was still a long way ahead. There was no howling of monkeys in the distance, no chattering of birds in the nearby trees. Through the open doorway there was not a glimmer of light in the sky.

During her first days at the camp, Leah had often been wide awake before daybreak, listening to the heavy thudding of ripe mangoes falling to the ground. She was eager for first light so that she could gather as much fruit as she could carry in the long skirt of her frock. But those days seemed to have happened to someone else. Leah moved swiftly across the dirt floor of the hut and stepped outside.

She stood still, looking towards the flickering firelight where a knot of people were gathered. Someone lay on a stretcher on the ground. Other people were moving in and out of the main hut which was much larger than the other huts scattered around the clearing. 'Not Will,' she said to herself. 'Not Will.'

Keeping to the shadows, she stepped into the hut used as a

cookhouse where her mother, Hannah, was kneading, lifting up the dough before slapping it down on a makeshift table.

Leah picked up a fraying straw fan from the ground and fanned the coals in the hearth until they glowed and the pinewood began to catch, the resin making popping noises and the piney smell filling the hut. The flames lit up the walls of palmetto poles tied securely together with dried tit-tie vines. Her mother's face was strained and frightened, her eyelids swollen from weeping. She looked exhausted; the deep line between her eyes seemed to have lengthened.

'Is it Will?' Leah asked. She hardly recognized her own voice. She licked her lips which felt dry.

'No,' her mother said. She began picking up bits of dough from the edges of the table. 'It's Daniel Sproate, the agent. He was chopped, I think, but I don't know for sure.'

Daniel Sproate, short, bow-legged and wiry, was in charge of Lawson's mahogany works and the slaves. Sproate was a quiet man with a quick temper and a quicker hand with a whip. Leah and Sam had stayed out of Sproate's way as much as they could, although their mother Hannah was not so fortunate.

On many Sunday mornings Daniel Sproate put on his best suit and placed his straw hat, stained with perspiration, on his stringy fair hair. For most of the day he sat beneath the mango trees writing in his memorandum books. For the remainder of the week, from sun-up to sun-down, he trekked through the bush with the few remaining slaves, searching for mahogany trees.

Hannah looked at Leah and her eyes seemed to grow smaller until they were almost shut. Her shoulders heaved and the silent tears coursed down her cheeks.

Leah put her arms around her mother and pulled her close, inhaling the smokiness of her hair and the odour of stale food on her clothing. She held her closer, resenting the reasons for the scent of rancid coconut oil, mingling with the smell of overripe guavas, emanating from her mother's armpits.

'Sit down, Ma. Sit,' Leah said, pushing her down onto a three-legged stool. Something terrible must have happened to make her mother give way like this. She took great pride in not letting anyone see her bow down to any kind of trouble. Over the years, Leah had watched her mother endure whippings on her bare back without crying out.

'Is he dead?' Leah asked, pouring water into a small calabash and giving it to her mother, who was trembling. Her forehead felt cold to Leah's touch.

'I haven't heard,' Hannah said. 'I don't want us to get in trouble for helping Will and Sharper.' She paused, putting her hand gently over Leah's mouth. Hannah held her head to one side, listening to the sounds outside.

Leah walked across the earthen floor, packed hard as stone, to peer cautiously through the doorway. 'It's Sam,' she said, watching her mother's shoulders sag with relief.

As Sam came through the door, he looked expectantly at his mother and then at Leah.

He scratched one arm as he asked, 'Did someone die?' His face was pinched, his eyes bleary from sleep. 'I was dreaming about Will.'

'No,' Leah said, 'Mr Lawson's agent is injured, or so Mama thinks. What did you dream?' One of their most enjoyable pastimes used to be relating their dreams to each other but now Sam said, 'I don't remember it much. Did they lose the fight?' He stood by the doorway staring at the group of men gathered near the fire and at the doorway of the main hut.

'No word yet,' Hannah said to Sam, putting an arm around his bare shoulders and pulling him gently away from the door. 'But I have a job for you and Leah.'

'What kind of job?' Sam asked, his dark eyes sombre. He was a tall, thin boy of about nine years old. He had a slight stutter and only spoke to strangers when it was unavoidable.

'Well, I've baked extra cakes for Will and Sharper. When it's daylight, you can go to the pond with Leah. He'll be around there somewhere,' Hannah replied.

'All right, Mam,' Sam said. 'But I heard there were soldiers in the bush now.'

'Probably just a rumour,' Hannah said. She filled two glasses with unsweetened tea from the big black kettle at one end of the fire hearth.

Leah and Sam took their tea and went to sit in a corner of the hut. Through the doorway, they could see the blazing fire in front of the hut in which Daniel Sproate was probably dying.

'If he dies, will they bury him here or in town?' Leah asked. She glanced at her mother, who was turning the small cakes in the huge black iron pot. Their fragrant smells made her mouth water. She could almost taste the flakiness of the baked dough, slightly salty on her tongue. She felt as though she could eat a hundred cakes rather than the two she was likely to receive.

'Oh, in town, I guess,' her mother replied. She shoved the burning wood further into the bed of glowing ashes in the hearth.

The fighting had been going on for many weeks now. Leah had lost track of which slaves were in revolt and which were fighting on the side of the masters. She thought of Will, wondering where he was and which side he had taken. He had been certain that, after it was all over, thousands of former slaves would be free to live in town, on the offshore islands or on faraway riverbanks where they could have small plantations and live in villages with others like themselves, the way the Maya Indians did.

She watched as her mother placed several cakes on the table. After she thought they had cooled sufficiently, Leah broke one open and placed it into Sam's hands. She watched the steam rising into the air. As she picked up another cake, inhaling the aroma, the commotion started in the clearing again. Someone shouted, 'He's gone.'

Hannah gave a brief cry then closed her eyes. 'Try to get back here as soon as you can,' she said to Leah and Sam. She pulled the kerchief off her head and wiped the sweat off her face. 'We'll need to accompany the body to Belize Town.'

Someone else was calling Hannah's name. As Hannah left the cookhouse and walked slowly across the clearing, Leah longed to accompany her mother, to help her in some way, but to follow her was impossible. Her mother would expect Leah to watch out for Sam and to carry on in the best way she could.

Her family was, she guessed, the rag-tag end of Graham Lawson's property in slaves which had once numbered between fifty and one hundred during the twenty or more years he had been in the settlement. Where he had lived before that and how he had lived nobody knew for sure, but this was not unusual.

The residents were not surprised when a new person, white or black, appeared on the Foreshore, on Front and Back Streets, on Northside or Southside, on the numerous rivers and creeks or in the mahogany camps and forests. There, as likely as not, one could meet Maya Indians walking to the river or a Spanish official going about Government business. The slaves, from different parts of Africa, and the various Indian groups lived their lives between the British and the Spanish, doing their best to survive from day to day.

To save money, Leah believed, and perhaps to avoid personal contact with her mother, Graham Lawson had for many years rented them out as domestic help. He lived as best he could on the income they provided him and on the proceeds from the dwindling stock in his shop. 'There is no market anymore for logwood,' she'd overheard Daniel Sproate say. 'No more credit in London until Lawson's debts are cleared.'

As Leah stood with Sam in the doorway, she rubbed the goose bumps on her arms. They watched their mother enter the main hut to help the other slaves prepare Daniel Sproate's body for the pit-pan journey downriver to Belize Town. Leah turned back into the hut. The acrid scent of the ashes in the smouldering hearth made her feel sick. She forced herself to place the pots of water her mother would need onto the iron bars of the hearth. Sam stoked the fire, adding sticks of pinewood until it was blazing. Neither she nor Sam was hungry any more and the johnny cakes had grown cold.

'Mr Sproate called them journey cakes, not johnny cakes,' Sam said, looking through the doorway. His face was drawn, his eyes shiny. 'Do you think Mr Sproate was right, Leah?'

'Maybe,' Leah said. She went to the door where he was now crouched staring at the hut in which Daniel Sproate had been laid out on his bush-bed, surrounded by firearms, powder, shot, cutlasses, imported brandy, Jamaican sugar and rum, patent medicines, his memorandum books and various other personal possessions.

'Let's get ready to go to the pine ridge,' she said to Sam. The sky had lightened and it would soon be daylight. 'We need to find Will and Sharper.'

'Aren't you afraid to go now, Leah?' Sam asked, helping her to tie the cakes into a cloth and to wrap stewed gibnut and spinach in fresh plantain leaves.

'I am,' Leah said. 'You?'

Sam nodded, then said, 'But I am willing to go.'

'All right,' Leah said, wondering how Graham Lawson would bear the sad news about his agent. 'We won't be gone long but we'd better take the machete in case of snakes and things.'

'Right,' Sam said, shouldering the bag which held food and water.

Hannah was still in the main hut when Leah and Sam walked to the path near the well. Leah remembered the family of deaf-mutes who had crossed their clearing several days before. She thought of Will and the gentleness in his voice when he'd asked her to be his sweetheart. She liked Will as her friend but she longed to be with Josiah again and to share with him all that had happened since she last saw him. It all seemed to have happened a long time ago.

As Leah and Sam walked along the narrow dirt path hedged by bushes and trees, the air became cooler, the leaves rustled and clouds blotted out the sun. The rain crashed down and in a moment Leah and Sam were drenched to the skin. Leah's frock felt plastered to her body and the brim of Sam's straw hat drooped under the weight of the downpour.

'It'll hold up soon. I can hear the falls,' Leah said over her shoulder. Sam walked behind her, his feet making sucking sounds in the mud.

The rain was letting up and above the dripping leaves of the forest trees they could hear the distant roar of water falling from a great height.

'Do you think we'll find Will there?' Sam asked. On the ground, rivulets of water eddied around their feet.

'I don't know but we can't stay out too long.'

She stopped and put her arms around Sam's shoulders. He was shivering. 'Maybe we should turn back, eh?'

Sam shook his head. 'I want to see Will, to give him the food as Mama said.' His teeth were chattering and Leah placed a wet hand on his forehead. He didn't seem to be starting a fever but they were both so wet she couldn't be sure.

It seemed like another hour had passed before they spotted the break in the bushes, near the entrance to the caves where Will and Sharper sometimes secretly met with their fellow woodcutters. As they wriggled through the narrow opening, they heard the sound of musket fire.

'Fighting,' Sam said, as they crouched together on the ground.

'Yes,' Leah replied, putting her hand over his lips.

Huddling together in the shelter of the trees which grew in a series of layers above them, they listened in fear to the renewed sounds of musket fire and the shouts of men rushing headlong through the undergrowth. They crept nearer to the bushes lining the banks of the pool below the entrance to the caves.

As they peered through the rain to the opposite bank, Leah saw Will stumble out of the bushes, blood streaming from his forehead. Across one shoulder he carried Sharper, who seemed unconscious. His right arm dangled at an awkward angle. Will gave a shrill whistle and plunged into the pool. A group of men gathered at the mouth of the cave and two of them swam swiftly towards them. They pulled Sharper through the murky water to the entrance of the cave. Moments later several black militia men in white trousers and red coats, led by a white officer, rushed out of the bushes near the pool.

In their midst was the youngest deaf-mute who had tried to befriend Leah near the well at Lawson's camp. Her mouth opened in horror as she saw the men at the entrance of the cave open fire and two militia men fall to the ground, their tall black hats rolling into the mud. Everything was silent for a moment. Leah and Sam looked at the young men stretched sideways on the forest floor. The mouth of the cave was now empty. Several militia men began dragging their dead comrades into the bush. Two others holding the deaf-mute began stumbling backwards, their guns pointing at the cave, until they reached the bushes and disappeared. Leah and Sam sat close together staring at the spot where the militia men fell, waiting to see if anyone would emerge from the cave, but no one did.

'Do you want me to whistle for Will?' Sam asked, his voice low and husky.

'No. It's too dangerous.' Her eyes burned from the tears she couldn't hold back. She said in his ear, 'We must never tell what we saw, do you understand?'

'I won't,' Sam said, wiping his face on his shirt. 'Can we make it back tonight?'

'We must.' She thought of her mother, who was keeping watch in Daniel Sproate's hut. Leah picked up the bundle of food and crept nearer the pool. She placed it on a rocky outcrop, hoping that Will would think it had been there all along. Then, beckoning to Sam, she moved silently into the bushes.

'I'll be glad to get back to town,' Sam said, slipping his hand into Leah's.

Leah nodded, feeling a little guilty, not wanting Sam to guess how excited she was at the thought of soon seeing Josiah again. In a few hours they would journey downriver in a large shaded pit-pan, with Daniel Sproate's body wrapped in sheets and protected by canvas.

She shivered and looked up at the sky which was now clear and studded with stars. She thought of the day Will had first shown her the caves, full of shining water and pillars of stone that looked like glass. Scattered on the floor were several old clay pots, many of them broken. Will told her that he had seen skeletons in one of the larger caves but she had refused to go any further with him.

Chapter 6

One dry day in the middle of the rainy season Will said, 'Sharper, I'm going to get away somehow.' They'd spent the previous days marking the new mahogany trees they'd found. Now they were helping to build scaffolding. It was about twelve feet high – people called it a 'barbeque'. The scaffolding was constructed around the girth of a mahogany tree that was about the width of ten or fifteen men standing shoulder to shoulder.

'You won't like it,' Sharper said. He was helping to cut stems and leaves from long tree branches, shaped like yokes. These yoke-shaped branches were used to hold up the planks of wood on which axe-men stood to cut down the tree. Like Will, Sharper was broad shouldered and muscular from working in the mahogany forests. Unlike Will, Sharper was short, stocky and bow-legged.

'Couldn't be worse than this.' Will gestured with the handle of his axe to the thick growth through which they pushed every day and at the high trees they climbed to scout out the elusive mahogany, scattered widely in hundreds of acres of forest where they encountered animals and birds but seldom any people.

It was frightening knowing they were alone and in danger from jaguars, snakes and insects. The howling of baboons which ate the figs in the trees hanging over the waterside often drowned out the noise of birds.

Sometimes, at the river, they met a few Maya Indians who looked at them with dark eyes set in faces devoid of animation. Will and Sharper would stare back at them with the same fascination and fear. However, as time went on, Will and Sharper began to understand that, if they were careful to maintain their distance, the Indians posed little threat to them.

'Escaping to the Spaniards is worse than this,' Sharper said, rubbing the stub of the index finger on his right hand. The finger had been shot off during their encounter with the militia.

'I must get away or I'll do them an injury in camp or at the house in Belize Town. Better to die on my own than let the magistrates hang me.' Will looked at Sharper's hand, remembering that during the flight from the militia, he had carried Sharper half a mile to the cave by the pool. Thirty slaves had taken three settlements up and down the river. Several white settlers had been killed but the militia and soldiers had defeated the slaves in the end.

'You might want to come back,' Sharper said, his smile a little wistful.

'I doubt it,' Will said. But looking at Sharper's crestfallen face, he realized he could never leave him behind. Sharper had told Will that he didn't remember anything about the time before he was brought to the Bay. People called him Sharper Saltwater, so he believed he must have been born at sea, although he had no memory of ever having a mother.

'Suppose you're shot or caught? Think about poor Buck. He got the cat-o'-nine-tails every day until he fell down dead. We would be dead too if Buck had squealed on us.'

Will thought of the nights when he and Sharper had crept into the ramshackle hut where Buck lay dying, to put water to his lips and to wash away the salt that had been poured into the bleeding wounds all over his body. 'I'll risk it,' Will said, 'if you come with me.'

Sharper shook his head. 'This is my home now, I've decided.' He leaned the yokes he'd cleaned against the tree trunks. 'I have children and there's my little trade.'

Late at nights in the bush when he couldn't sleep, Will sat by the fire watching Sharper carve miniature doreys and flat-bottomed pit-pans with bits of ragged cloth for awnings. In the boats he placed carved figures holding paddles or poling along an imaginary river. Whenever they were in town Sharper sold his carvings to people on the streets, exchanged them for goods of various kinds, or gave them as gifts to his children who lived in the slave quarters on the back streets of Belize Town.

'I'll do something,' Will said, placing his yokes next to Sharper's. Will unhooked the bundle of food from a branch and handed it to him.

'That's so,' Sharper said, evenly dividing the salted pork and flat bread into two pieces of tarpaulin. He tied them neatly together with the tit-tie vines which lay plentifully around the ground. Tomorrow the dried vines would be used to secure the various parts of the scaffolding. 'You always do something, Will.'

'Something in me, I guess,' Will said, thinking of the dead militia soldiers and the danger they would have been in if Buck had betrayed them. He thought too of Hannah's bundle of food, which he had found outside the cave near the pond on the night of the fighting in which Sharper had been wounded. He wondered if Leah had witnessed his swim with Sharper, across the pond to the mouth of the cave. Had she seen the runaway slaves shoot the two militia men? Will shook his head, trying not to think of the militia men dragging their dead comrades and the deaf-mute into the dense bushes around the pond. Will hoped that the deaf-mute had been able to rejoin his family, that they had managed to reach Belize Town and bought a passage on the first ship sailing away from the settlement. If Will had been in their position, that's what he would have done.

'I wish it wasn't there,' Sharper said. He looked at Will thoughtfully, his eyes sorrowful. 'We all hurt inside but it's worse with you.'

Like Sharper, most people hated to talk about the terrible things that had been done to them. They lived with the knowledge of what they themselves had done to others and continued to do in their desperate struggle to survive, to avoid the cow-skin whips or the jail. During their lifetimes, if they had not been dragged through the streets of the town by a mule and cart, had not died from hard labour in the bush, were not mutilated, crippled or murdered, were not hung, drawn, quartered and burnt, many slaves thanked their lucky stars, trying to ignore their feelings of guilt.

'I wish I was different,' Will said, not meeting his gaze. 'But I'm not.' He picked at a broken front tooth with a sliver of wood, examined the scab on his ankle and silently cursed the militia. Since their unexpected encounter with the soldiers in the bush, something in Will had altered. He couldn't put his finger on what it was but it had happened. He felt uneasy, anxious, unable to appreciate everyday joys, like seeing a flock of green parrots flying overhead, Sharper's companionship, or thinking about the day when Leah would agree to be his sweetheart. His love for her was now tainted with the fear of what she might have seen. Would she be loyal to him? And to Sharper?

'Wish you wouldn't try it,' Sharper said again, beginning to gather up his tools.

'We could,' Will said, 'try to get away together.' His mental survival, Will sometimes thought, depended on trying to hold fast to the memories of his life before he had been brought by ship from Africa to Jamaica and then to the Bay of Honduras. Will wanted to share these thoughts with his friend but Sharper didn't like to hear about what he called 'those days long done and long gone'.

Will thought of his friend, old Congo Jack, who usually sat on a three-legged stool outside the large double-doors of Graham Lawson's shop. Congo Jack had been more than just a friend to Will when he had arrived in the settlement, disoriented and half-crazed with grief. Jack had been like a father to him, helping him to survive from day to day. He explained to him the laws and customs of the Bay, told him stories about his own life and listened to Will's stories. Will longed to see Congo Jack again and to ask him for advice.

'I'm not leaving,' Sharper said. 'I am saving to free my sons.'

'Seems to me like you could try it, Sharper. Almost every day you hear about one runaway or another.' Will thought about the story he had heard about the escape of two thousand slaves during a Spanish attack on the settlement, but that was a long time ago and he didn't know if it was true.

'I'll help you get away, Will, if you want to go,' Sharper said.

'You would?'

'I would,' Sharper said. He pulled his machete out of the tree trunk. Giving a bundle of food to Will, Sharper shouldered his own bundle, then his gun. He shoved his machete into the leather sheath at his waist. 'We'd better get a march on,' Sharper said. 'Dover and the other fellows will be waiting in camp for us. Isn't this the week for fresh rations?'

Will shrugged. 'We'll get there before dark.'

'I could do with some roast gibnut washed down with rum, couldn't you?' Sharper asked.

'Maybe we can catch one along the way,' Will said, but he didn't really feel like hunting, which was another strange thing.

Sharper unsheathed his machete and gave a preliminary slash at the tangle of bush, high grass and vines. Will listened to the ring and scrape of the blade as Sharper began clearing the path through the forest. Overhead, sunlight streamed through a broken canopy of towering trees. Blinded momentarily by the light, Will wiped the water streaming from his eyes.

He seemed to have lost confidence in himself and he knew that Sharper was his main defence for a while against the dangers of the forest. Sharper was older, more skilled, more experienced but now lacking the essential requirement of a huntsman, the necessary strength in his right hand. During the previous weeks, Will had helped Sharper as much as possible and

45

so far his secret seemed safe from the others.

That day as he and Sharper trekked through the forest, Will tried to go back over his rag-bag of jumbled memories and thoughts. Memories he'd taken for granted, convinced that they would never fade, were becoming blurred, indistinct, especially the faces he'd watched at night through the haze of smoke from his mother's cooking fire.

As Will seemed to remember it, his had not been an unusual life. What was unusual to him was the life he led now, one to which he was unable to accustom himself, though he kept trying. His attempts at accommodation usually petered out after a few weeks or sometimes months, depending on the provocation. Their recent defeat by the masters seemed almost more than he could bear. His dreams of a plot of farmland by the river, several large huts and the children that he and Leah would someday have now seemed as unattainable as ever.

Chapter 7

In the late afternoon, as Will and Sharper continued their trek through the bush, they emerged into a large clearing in which there were several abandoned huts. The clearing reminded Will of the last year he had spent as a boy in his own village. He and his mother had shared the necessary daily chores, walking back and forth on the cracked earth of their compound under the burning sun.

He remembered the red clay earth. He could almost see it, even feel it on the soles of his feet. He could easily conjure up the huge trees in the shade of which he had played as a boy. At night, in good harvest years, there was the sound of drums, the smell of palm oil bubbling in a pan and the taste of groundnut stew with balls of pounded yams which he popped into his mouth, making each one last as long as possible.

That final day he and his mother had eagerly scanned the sky hoping that they would see gathering rain clouds. In his memory, that terrible day was as dry as the others that year. Will's father had died the year before and, as he had not favoured his third wife (Will's mother), she feared that without his minimal protection harm would come to them from others in the village.

'We have many enemies,' she'd said, holding up her small hands, her fingers splayed wide. His father, after this late marriage, had not often visited Will's mother. Will knew this was the reason why he didn't have brothers or sisters. During the short time his father was alive, their enemies had not mattered so very much for he'd made sure they received generous rations. Now, in the face of drought, hunger stalked the village and they were afraid.

At the time he did not understand why the men of their village did not travel through the bush to find food. He understood now, of course. There had been famine everywhere. What food the village had was grudgingly shared with them. That last day he had said to his mother, 'Let us go to your family village.'

'We shall do so,' she'd agreed.

'Let's go on a boat,' he'd said, delighting in the idea of the village markets they would see along the way.

'We'll have to trek,' his mother had said. 'We have only a little money left for food.'

Neither of them had ever gone any great distance from his father's compound, except on special days when there was dancing, feasting and drumming in nearby villages to thank the gods for rain or for a good harvest.

Long before the next sunrise, however, the decision had been taken out of their hands. While they slept, men had crept across the hard earth floor of their hut. His mother had shouted his name once, before she'd been gagged and bound as he had already been. His eyes were roughly blindfolded and he and his mother were pushed out of their home and into the night.

They had walked many miles for most of the day, yoked in a convoy with other people. He'd been forbidden to speak, even to his mother, when they were allowed to rest and eat the meagre rations handed out to them. Eventually they had been led into a dark prison beneath the earth where the men were separated from the women and he had never seen his mother again.

'We're nearly there now,' Sharper said. 'Feeling better?' He made his way to the river and stared down at the giant mahogany logs. They had been moved there during the dry season, late at night, pulled by straining oxen on logging sleds, their way lighted by dozens of flaring pinewood torches held aloft by sweating naked slaves.

'Yes,' Will said, picking up a cohune pod from the hundreds littering the ground and breaking it open to taste the nutty flavour. He dived into the water and as he surfaced, he looked up at the soaring trees. It seemed to him that the memory of his mother's face had blended with Leah's and his heart beat faster as he thought of their last meeting at Lawson's Camp. 'I'll do it in the Christmas season,' he said out loud. 'I'll ask her again when we go to town.'

Will did not like the annual river trip to Belize Town, built on low, swampy ground near the sea. He preferred working upriver in the rolling hill country, where he could glimpse the blue mountains in the distance. He climbed out of the water, feeling buoyed up by the thought of Leah. He smiled, wondering what Sharper would think after all his talk about escaping across the border. If Leah accepted him, he doubted he would ever again want to leave the settlement.

'Let's get going,' Sharper said. He did not like swimming.

As they walked quickly towards the camp, the rain poured down. The trees that lined both sides of the river were pushed downwards by the ferocious wind, their heavy branches trailing in the rushing water. Will and Sharper dashed to the makeshift thatched huts where the slaves were sheltering from the rain. Wiping his face with his hands, Will looked up to see six uniformed militia men standing at the back of the shelter with Dover, the head huntsman.

'Here they are now,' Dover said, placing his straw hat on his bald head and pointing to Will and Sharper. 'These are the men I told you about. They shoot as well as they paddle.'

'You there,' the first soldier said to Will and Sharper. 'Get into the pit-pan. Look sharp.'

Will's heart was beating rapidly. He looked at Sharper and saw the fright on his face. Had somebody betrayed them after all? He thought of Leah but rejected the thought. She would never turn them in, neither would Sam or Hannah.

'Now, sir?' Will asked, looking out at the rain, the river and the oncoming night. Earlier that afternoon a pit-pan had been hauled up onto the bank and several slaves were preparing to shove the long flat-bottomed boat back into the turbulent water.

'This rain will soon pass over,' the first soldier said, mopping his forehead. 'We must make a start before nightfall.'

Will and Sharper walked to the riverbank and helped to get the boat into the river. They were silent, listening to the others who grumbled between clenched teeth.

The militia men climbed into the boat and Will and Sharper received orders from the officer to paddle to Belize Town. After listening for a while, Will began to understand that the militia men were talking quite openly about preparations in the settlement for another Spanish attack.

Chapter 8

BELIZE TOWN, AUGUST 1798

Dawn was breaking when Will began shuffling through the seaweed fringes on the Foreshore to take a dip in the sparkling sea. The waves, lapping gently against his body, seemed to ease his aching muscles. His spirits revived and his mind began to clear. The grandeur of the sea filled him with a familiar melancholy which made him long to be back upriver. It was Saturday and he had a few hours free. 'I'll spend some time with Congo Jack,' he thought to himself. 'I'll ask his advice about Leah.'

Some of his fellow slaves, even Sharper, were enthusiastically throwing themselves into preparations for the upcoming struggle of settlers against the Spanish but he felt ambivalent about the entire enterprise. The failed attempt at an uprising by a small band of slaves, in which he had played a part, was still fresh in his mind. Their defeat by the settlers and the militia still stung and he lived with the fear that he or Sharper would be betrayed by someone in the crowds of people milling around the town. He hoped that the deaf-mute who might have recognized him had left the settlement with his family. Many others had left when news of this latest threat of a Spanish attack – by land and by sea – had reached the town.

He watched the brown pelicans swooping down to the surface of the sea, scooping up fish to eat and to store in the pouches beneath their long beaks. Black man-o-war birds with deeply forked tails and enormous wingspans soared above the shoreline. Will was relieved to be alone for a little while, away from the other pit-pan paddlers and the militia, who were now also acting as night-guards. The journey downriver to Belize Town, with only a few hours' rest, had been exhausting. He looked out to sea, beyond the mangrove islands, where sloops, schooners and a gun brig were anchored. Soon he and Sharper would be sailing to St George's Caye on Thomas McGilvrey's sloop. The settlers and slaves had been instructed by the Commander-in-Chief to burn down the houses and huts on the island to deprive the enemy of food-stores and of shelter. The casks of rain water were to be sent to Belize Town or destroyed.

As he waded ashore, Will avoided the watchful eyes of two militia men, muskets at the ready, parading up and down the street. At night, the volunteer settlers also helped to guard all seagoing craft so that the slaves could not escape to distant offshore islands. Will walked around two muzzle-loading cannons mounted on wheels, with cannon balls piled between them. He crossed the street to the corner of the lane near Lawson's compound.

Outside the gate, beneath the shade of two soaring royal palms, Marshall Lawson, Graham Lawson's son, had set up his easel. It was the first time Will had seen him up close. He sat on a straight-backed chair facing the sea where he could see the droghers loaded with timber, sloops, schooners and gun-flats gathering in the harbour. Marshall was settling his wide-brimmed straw hat more securely on his long, brown hair. On a small table beside him were memorandum books and foreign newspapers. As Will passed through the wide gates he said, 'Morning, sir,' picking up a slender book that had fallen on the grass and handing it to him.

'Ahem,' Marshall Lawson said, continuing to mix his paints on a palette. He cleared his throat. 'Place it on the table. Thank you.'

Will did as he was told, thinking that the tall, thin, delicate-looking man was probably glad of a break from trekking with slaves through the dense bush from sun-up to sun-down.

He thought of giving the young man a little information about the bush, from his own experience. Then he shrugged and entered the compound where Graham Lawson's large white house stood in the shadow of coconut palms, tamarind and mango trees. Built close to the shore, the house, like many of the neighbouring homes, had a shingled roof and was constructed of mahogany and raised high on sapodilla posts.

At sunset the evening before, Will had been leaning against a wall of the house when he'd heard Thomas McGilvrey and Graham Lawson talking. They were drinking on the verandah, which was shaded by stephanotis, jasmine and other climbing plants that perfumed the air.

'Your mahogany and logwood banks are more valuable than any gold mine, Graham. How will you square things with your son? He seems like a decent fellow.'

'Marshall hasn't been here long. Already he hates the place and everyone in it. Sometimes I think he hates me, blames me for bringing his mother out here. You may remember she died from malaria when Marshall was away at school. Not many white women can take it out here.'

'I'm sorry to hear that,' McGilvrey said. 'Still, he might cause difficulties with magistrates and all that. They seem to think alike on mahogany matters, who is in and who is out, that kind of thing.'

Will heard Graham Lawson coughing. He hawked and spat several times over the verandah railing. They were quiet for a while before Graham Lawson said, 'Marshall is here out of a mistaken sense of duty. He's urging me to sell the lot, always talking about buying a cottage in some rural area of Scotland. He wants to marry, I think. I want to get back to Edinburgh while my strength holds. Marshall and I will have more than enough to live on.'

'I don't want to make an enemy of your son. He seems to have a lot of friends here,' Thomas McGilvrey said.

'Oh well, I've given him a handsome start upriver but I doubt he'll stick with it. His idea of living in the tropics is reading poetry on the verandah here or painting seascapes, bush plants and suchlike. Not much of a painter mind you, not like his mother was.'

'I can wait a bit longer for payment if you're short of sterling – I prefer it. Maybe I can continue here for a while and billet a few of my men in your huts at the back of the garden?'

'You're welcome to stay but don't say later that I didn't offer to pay you. There won't be much profit for a while if the Spaniards attack by land. The whole place will be burnt to the ground, my mahogany and logwood warehouses included, and the slaves will make for the border, you mark my words. It'll be brutal starting over again.'

'I'm not squeamish, as you know, Graham. Like your son I voted to stand and fight.'

'And I voted to scuttle. As for Marshall, that's the kind of gesture he likes to make. He thinks war is romantic and all that rot. I still think we should cut our losses and leave. That's water under the bridge, however. We're all in for it now.'

'Shoulder to shoulder and we'll win through. I want to make my fortune here and spend it exploring the area. There are some interesting sights to the north and west of us, or so I've heard, ancient Indian ruins and so on. I might even find treasure buried in Maya Indian graves.'

'You are an enterprising fellow, Thomas. Not too much troubled by nerves or scruples yet, eh? I've lost mine, I'm afraid.'

'Well, we've had some good times while I've been here. I'll miss you. I'll continue handling things upriver until you are better and then we'll settle up, one way or another, once the skirmishes with the Spanish are over.'

'Good of you,' Lawson said. 'We've had some good evenings, but the gambling is over for me. Not up to much these days. Marshall watches me like a hawk.'

Will had moved away from the wall when he heard the first ring of the dinner bell. He'd heard the scrape of chairs against the verandah floor as the men rose and went indoors.

Lawson and McGilvrey's conversation filled his mind with hope and excitement as he continued walking down the lane. Graham Lawson, Leah's father, and Thomas McGilvrey were planning to join forces. Will felt sure McGilvrey would be pleased if Leah agreed to be his sweetheart and came to live with him in the Lawson compound. He couldn't wait to talk with Congo Jack. Will could see him sitting on his three-legged stool in his customary place near Graham Lawson's shop.

The old man wore the cast-off clothing of the merchants along the nearby streets who hoped he would keep an eye on their various enterprises and inform them of anything they ought to know for the security of their goods and chattels. There was no official police force in the settlement so Graham Lawson and the other merchants had provided Congo Jack with a wooden policeman's rattle. But no merchant could remember Congo Jack ever using the rattle to warn them about the robberies, fights, assaults, slave escapes and even murders that sometimes occurred on the streets and alleyways near where he was allowed to make his base outside Graham Lawson's shop.

Will thought that Jack, tall and almost entirely bald, was perhaps over sixty years old. He wore, as he nearly always did, an old straw hat. The brim was sewn onto the crown with twine normally used to mend fishing nets – one of Jack's occupations when the rheumatism in his fingers was not too severe. It always sobered Will to know that Jack usually slept near his base outside the shop; from there he had a wide view of the open sea. Congo Jack was free but destitute and Will wondered if that would be his own fate.

The upstairs verandah, like many others, jutted out over the shop premises, so Jack was able to shelter from sunshine and from rain. Will had spent many nights with Jack. Together they'd spread an old canvas sail on the red bricks of Graham Lawson's shop front and over the sail, dirty, tattered blankets which Jack's sailor acquaintances had given him over the years.

'Hello Papa Jack,' Will said, giving him a warm embrace, smelling his familiar scent of sweat, tea and tobacco. For several seasons, at various mahogany works upriver, Will had watched Congo Jack standing on high platforms, swinging a heavy axe to help cut down enormous trees. To Will he'd seemed so strong, so courageous in the face of his dangerous occupation. 'How are you feeling?'

'Not bad. I still have the pain in my joints of course but my eyes are good enough to mend the nets.'

'I'm glad to hear that, Papa,' Will said, sitting cross-legged on the ground beside him.

'They pay me in fish so I don't go hungry. I've got a fresh turtle fin, coco-yams and a negro yam. We could cook a boil-up. But you can't hang about on a busy day like this, I expect.'

'A boil-up sounds great,' Will said. 'I haven't had anything to eat as yet.' Will was not hungry. He longed for mug after mug of strong, sweet tea. But he would share whatever Jack offered.

'Get the yams out of my sack,' Congo Jack said, lifting the turtle fin from a pan of water.

'All right,' Will said, carefully emptying the contents of the sack onto the red brick entryway to Graham Lawson's shop, closed now because of the emergency. Will found the small coco-yams wrapped in Jack's extra shirt and the large negro yam and a plantain in a pair of ragged trousers. He sorted through Jack's meagre stores of salt, tea and sugar, hot peppers, tobacco, various bits of cloth and a battered tin cup, until he found a broken-handled knife, sharpened on two sides.

As Will began peeling the yams and the green plantain, he said to Jack, 'Papa, I need your advice.'

'I could tell by your face that something is on your mind,' Congo Jack said, placing the can of water to boil on bricks over a small fire. They were now in Graham Lawson's yard, covered with white shell-sand. 'Advice about what?'

'I wanted to talk with you about Leah. You know how I feel about her.'

'Does she feel the same way about you?' Congo Jack asked, a look of amused affection on his face.

'I'm not sure. I hope so,' Will said, knowing that men like himself had a hard time competing for sweethearts against the mahogany owners who could offer slave women positions as housekeepers, a position in the settlement which was profitable and prestigious. There were very few eligible women in the settlement, white or black, as the merchants bought mostly male slaves who could work in the forests.

Congo Jack put the yams, fish, plantain and peppers into the pan of boiling water. Without looking at Will, he said, 'I've watched her grow up. I'm not sure she's the right sweetheart for you.'

'Why do you say that, Papa?' Will asked, trying to keep his voice steady as he handed the knife to Congo Jack and replaced his other possessions in the sack.

'Oh, I can tell by the cut of her jib. Leah has Lawson's name and she's not bad-looking. She'll be hoping for freedom and marriage.'

'She told me she doesn't want to be anybody's sweetheart. I'd try to marry her, Papa.' Will thought Leah was very good-looking but he not did say this to Congo Jack, who would tease him about it each time they met.

'You are a good huntsman, one of the best. Thomas McGilvrey wouldn't give you the permission you need as a slave and he certainly won't free you to get married. I've only known of two or three times in my life where that has happened. And your children would be slaves – have you thought about that?'

'Not if I can buy my freedom, and Leah's.'

'I've been down that road,' Congo Jack said, 'as you know.'

Will was silent for a while, looking at Congo Jack, who had removed the turtle fin and the yams from the water and placed them on a large plantain leaf. Will watched the steam rising from the food, thinking about the mother of Congo Jack's children, who had died giving birth to his fourth child. Two of his daughters had died in infancy and Congo Jack had assisted his remaining children – two sons – to escape to the Spanish border as soon as they had reached manhood.

'Did you ever receive word from your sons?' Will asked as they began eating.

Congo Jack probably could have escaped himself but he had stayed behind to put their pursuers off the track. It was all he'd had to give to his sons and he had given it without a moment's regret.

Congo Jack shook his head. 'But I hope they are free and living as best they can,' he said, offering Will a drink of water.

Will accepted the large calabash and took several sips as he thought about what Congo Jack had said to him.

'What will you do, Papa Jack, if the Spanish attack the town by land or if they come down Haulover Creek?'

'If the worst comes to the worst I'm planning to go up the Sibun River, to people I know at Freetown. I hear they're taking people in.'

'Good,' Will said. 'Then if you're not hereabouts, I'll know where to find you.' He kissed the old man's hand before putting a small leather pouch of coins in his lap.

Jack looked down at the money for a long while before placing it carefully into his sack. 'You'll never manage to purchase your freedom if you keep giving away your money,' he said. He was trying to sound severe but Will saw tears fill Jack's eyes. 'I'll keep it safe for you,' he said, rubbing his fingers along a long pole which lay on the ground beside his bare feet – it was shaped like a 'Y' at one end.

'I have a gift for you,' Congo Jack said, placing the pole into

58

Will's hand. 'Every time you use it on the Spanish, remember that I am counting on you to come back alive. Promise?'

'I promise – to try anyway,' Will said, feeling a constriction in his throat as he grasped tightly the pole which Congo Jack referred to as his 'yoke-wood'. Will knew that Jack was so used to carrying the pole around with him that he did not automatically recall those long-ago days and nights when he had marched through the forests in Africa, his neck yoked to the necks of others in a similar plight.

The pole, however, had an everyday use other than that of defending himself against man and beast. He also used it to hold up a clothesline which he rigged up every Sunday morning to the rear of Graham Lawson's yard, after rinsing his clothes out in the creek.

'I'm proud of you Will,' Congo Jack said. 'I've seen many fine fellows like you die in these wars between the British and Spanish. I hate to think of you in the midst of all that grapeshot and those sharp blades, but it's all I'll think about 'till I see you again.'

He pulled a packet wrapped in cloth from an inner pocket and opened it out carefully on one knee. 'Have you ever seen my free paper?'

Will shook his head, unable to say the words that were in his heart.

'Well, this is what it looks like,' Congo Jack said. 'I want you to stay alive to get one. Have you learnt to read yet?'

Will shook his head. 'What does it say, Papa Jack?' he asked, thinking about the battle that had probably started around Caye Chapel and the islands near St George's Caye. The skirmishes would probably continue for days and the settlers were poorly equipped for battle unless the British Governor sent help from Jamaica.

'It says on the first page that I am forever set free from all manner of slavery whatsoever,' Congo Jack said, peering down at the paper. He read, 'Honduras, 1794, I, William Crosbie, do swear upon the Holy Evangelists of Almighty God that I was personally present and did see John Garnett sign, seal and deliver the foregoing manumission and receipt for the uses, intents and purposes therein mentioned. So help me God.'

'Will you teach me to read a little when I get back, Papa Jack?' Will asked.

'I offered to teach you many times,' Congo Jack said. 'But better late than never, eh?'

'See you soon, Papa,' Will said, getting to his feet.

'Are you going to say your farewells to Leah now?' Congo Jack asked.

'No,' Will replied, 'I'll think about what you said.' He waved to Jack as he turned onto the Foreshore and began walking swiftly towards Thomas McGilvrey's sloop. He forced himself to focus on the reality of the Spanish attack. He decided to spend the afternoon trying to learn as much as he could from the boatmen who had been sailing back and forth from St George's Caye to Belize Town with warnings about the Spanish preparations for battle.

Chapter 9

BELIZE TOWN, AUGUST 1798
LEAH

Leah and her brother Sam were out on Haulover Creek in a leaky dorey, borrowed from the nightwatchman at the home of the merchant brothers where their mother was working as an assistant to the cook. Sam's short pants were held up by a length of strong cord and he wore a coarse linen shirt which was torn at the elbow. They were both soaking wet and the stench from the creek water around the mangrove roots, and from the oysters and crabs they had collected, clung to their skin and their clothing.

Leah fretted about Sam. She hoped that he wouldn't get a chill. People seemingly hale and hearty often died quickly from malaria and a host of other mysterious maladies, so she kept a sharp lookout for the onset of any sneezing or sniffling on his part. Sam was becoming a tall, strong, dependable young man. However, ever since the day they had walked to the caves in the pouring rain to find Will, he had been prone to stomach upsets, colds and sometimes fever.

Although it was often in their minds, Leah and Hannah seldom discussed the possibility that Sam would one day, perhaps soon, be sent to a bank upriver to help trim leaves and branches from felled mahogany trees, or to learn how to build crib-like rafts from cabbage palms. During the rainy season these were used to transport logwood, heavy as stone, downriver to the sea.

She listened to the scrabbling of the crabs in the baskets wedged in the bow of the tiny boat. The sound grated on her nerves, reminding her of her mother's warning that crabs that walked too far were sure to lose their claws.

Leah knew that her mother felt she spent too much of her Saturday free time drifting along the creek with Sam or walking about the town. Hannah often said that if Leah continued in this way, she was bound to get into trouble.

Before they'd left their room that morning, Hannah had said to Leah, 'Mind me, Leah. Come straight to Mr Angas's house, no dilly-dallying along the way. And before you reach the Potts' house, please cross to the other side of the street. Do you hear me? I don't want any more complaints about you and that Mr Josiah.'

'Yes, Mama,' Leah had said, fearing as much as her mother that, even with the preparations for the Spanish attack going on, they could be sent upriver again. Hannah's face had looked strained in the light of the kerosene lamp in their room and her voice was unusually high.

Leah looked up at the sky, which was lightening fast. She and Sam were poling the dorey towards Belize Town. They were a few feet away from mangrove roots rising in grotesque shapes out of the murky water. They poled for about a mile until they reached the centre of town. There the creek emptied into the sea which glimmered and glittered in the distance. They were headed towards a pier beyond the Court House. Most of the houses and warehouses on both sides of the creek were still in shadow, except here and there where a moving candle or a lamp revealed that people were already up and about, getting ready for the day.

As they neared the market, Leah watched the shadowy figures of vendors and boatmen unloading goods from sailing boats, doreys, mules and carts. Oil lamps stood on the ground amongst some of the sacks, baskets and bottles. Other vendors were setting out their wares by the light of hurricane lanterns. The sailors and fishermen still held lighted pinewood torches aloft as they steered their boats from the open sea to the market, situated not far from the Court House where the creek met the sea.

Night had turned to day by the time Sam pulled the dorey alongshore. He tied it to a thick post buried deep in the muck of the creek bottom, near the warehouse of the merchant brothers.

They walked quickly across the wide slats of the wooden pier until they reached the roadside covered with broken sea shells.

As Leah and Sam approached the alleyway leading to the rear of the house where the kitchen was situated, they saw a man lying on the ground amidst discarded turtle and conch shells that littered the roadway. As he tried to rise, nearly a dozen John Crow birds flew away to perch on nearby fences and on the pier, waiting for a chance to continue feeding on the intestines of fish, chickens and other animals which had been flung onto the growing pile. The stench of rotting fish and meat was almost unbearable, especially during the hottest part of the day or whenever the wind blew it down the streets and through the windows and doors of the fine houses by the sea.

The man caught sight of them as they approached and he called out to them, shouting and cursing as he struggled to get his bearing on the slippery mass. As they drew nearer they saw that his eyes were bloodshot, his black coat and trousers were muddy and his neckerchief was nowhere to be seen. The whiteness of his neck contrasted strangely with his tanned, leathery face. He was of medium height, broad shoulered and with a considerable paunch which strained against the brass buttons of his coat.

'You there,' he said to them, 'give me a hand. Don't stand there gawking. Hurry up now.'

Leah took the basket Sam held so that he could get a better grip on the man's forearm. She tried not to meet his eyes, which shimmered like sunshine on the green bottles in the apothecary shop where her half-sister, Sukie, worked. But each time Leah raised her eyes, she saw his fixed on her as though slightly surprised.

'Well,' the man said, 'I suppose you two are glad of a frolic, I'm sure. Anything to get out of work, eh?' He looked towards the mangrove islands where the batteries were being erected at Grand Bogue, as though he expected that the lighters and other boats loaded with men and carronades would somehow have disappeared.

'Do you want us to go with you to your house, sir?' Sam asked. 'Or we could bring someone here with your horse.'

The man laughed. It sounded like a low growl. 'Horse eh?' he said, narrowing his eyes against the sun, which was now sparkling on the gentle waves. 'Not likely, I'm not a rich man.'

Leah looked at Sam, who was smiling slightly. This last remark must have seemed farcical to him. Sam could sometimes see a funny side to some of the most desperate situations in which they often found themselves. The idea that the man had no money also seemed ludicrous to Leah, who saw that his fine clothes were like those of other wealthy mahogany merchants. He wore a gold ring on the little finger of his right hand. A gemstone, perhaps a diamond, sparkled as he raised his hand to stroke the stubble on his face.

'We'll get you home, mister. Won't we, Leah? Tell us where you live.'

She stood still, watching the man peer at Sam more closely; then he turned to look at Leah.

'So you would, I'll be bound,' he said, walking a few steps closer to where Leah stood. 'Your face is familiar. What's your name?'

'Leah, sir,' she said, looking at the shell sand on the ground – not wanting to be accused of insolence, insubordination or any of the other myriad offences with which she could be legally charged. 'Sam here, he's my brother.'

'Well, girl, what other name do you go by?'

'We go by Mr Graham Lawson's name, sir.'

'Graham Lawson, eh?' the man asked, staring at her fixedly. 'Well, well.' He rubbed the stubble on his chin then looked back at the pile of stinking rubbish in which he had lain. 'I seem to remember walking on the pier,' he said.

'You must have slipped, sir,' Sam said. 'It's very oily at the edge.'

'Must have been drunk,' the man said. 'But better sleeping on a dung heap than drowning in the sea, eh?' He looked at Leah. 'What do you say?'

'You had good luck, sir,' Leah said, thinking that people had been murdered on the Foreshore for a lot less than fine clothing and a gold ring. She doubted that he'd lain there for very long.

As Leah and Sam began edging their way past him, the man asked, 'What do you have in those baskets? Open the lids, boy, let me have a look.'

'Few oysters, few crabs, sir,' Sam said. 'They're for Mr Angas and his brother. Our mother cooks there.'

'Angas brothers, eh?' He turned to Leah. 'Fresh oysters,' he said. 'Where did you get them?'

'From the creek, sir. Would you like some? We have more than enough,' she said, hoping the man would not take any offence at the offer.

The man laughed again, slapping his sides as though he'd heard a funny joke. 'Well, thank you,' he said, walking nearer to where they stood. 'If you are sure you have enough for Messrs Angas and Company.'

'Quite sure, sir,' Sam said, his face becoming a little sombre.

Leah thought of Sam plunging his body again and again into the creek to find the oysters and crabs, throwing them into the dorey for her to put into the baskets when she wasn't bailing water out of the leaky boat.

'Well,' the man said, 'I don't need any crabs. But on a morning like this a few oysters might do me good.' He lifted the brim of Leah's straw hat and peered down into her face. 'Lawson to the life,' he said. 'Well, well, well. I hope we'll meet again under better circumstances.'

'Yes, sir,' Sam said, 'We're around, here and there. Bye now, sir.'

'Bye, bye, sir,' Leah said, delighted that the man had taken so few oysters from the basket. They watched him remove his jacket and sling it across his shoulders. He walked away slowly, holding the black hat with the oysters under one arm. Leah felt they had got off lightly. He hadn't accused them of anything, like stealing his missing neckerchief for example, which someone had probably done while he had lain amongst the turtle shells in a drunken stupor.

'Let's go, Sam,' she said, pulling down the brim of her hat and hoping that Sam would not notice the tears that, for no real reason, had suddenly sprung into her eyes. She hadn't realized how tense she had been during the past few minutes.

Sam slipped his hand into hers and gave it a squeeze. He kicked at the stones in the road, then picked one up and threw it far out to sea. 'I wish that was him,' he said, as the stone disappeared beneath the waves.

'He wasn't all that bad,' Leah said. 'He didn't hit us or anything.'

'I thought he was going to cuff my ear,' Sam said. 'I heard the sleeve of his jacket tear when I pulled him up.'

'Perhaps we looked happy today when he is so drunk and sad. What do you think?'

Sam shrugged. 'Well, it is our free day,' he said. 'We don't get many.' He tugged at her hand. 'Let's duck quickly down the alley,' he said, 'just in case he turns around and tries to commandeer the rest.' They both laughed at the ridiculous idea.

As they scurried towards the mouth of the alley, Leah saw the man stumbling and staggering towards the pier on which they had recently walked. They'd been feeling so happy that their foray to the mangroves had been successful. The oysters and crabs they had gathered would free their mother of the worry of cooking enough food for themselves and for others, black and white. Many people were destitute in the month which people called the 'mauger season', when the days were hot and humid, and food was scarce.

An unusual sound caused Leah and Sam to turn their heads to look back at the man. The seat of his black trousers was caked with mud. They paused to listen as he began singing at the top of his voice,

'To die in a pub is my definite plan,
With my mouth to the tap, just
As close as I can.
Then the angels would say
When the singing began
Oh, Lord, show mercy
To this boozy man.'

He continued singing as he walked along the pier and Leah marvelled at the difference in his voice. By now she knew from experience that one can often seem to be made of several people. She was the same herself. Still she never would have suspected that this man had such a sweet singing voice and that she, so used to harshness and rough living, would be so touched by a drunken man's song.

Chapter 10

Leah, coffee pot in hand, paused on the long wooden bridge between the kitchen and the main house. From there she had a fine view of the sea to the horizon. She breathed in deeply, inhaling the heady scent of freshly brewed coffee. She prayed with all her being that the Baymen and slaves would be able to hold back the Spanish or that their mighty ships would be wrecked on the barrier reefs. Shipwrecks frequently happened, as the channels through the reefs were tricky and hard to find without a local pilot to steer a way into the relatively shallow harbour.

Down below at the water's edge, groups of people stood about waiting for news of their loved ones and friends, many of whom would die or be wounded or maimed. She lingered for a few more minutes, scanning the crowd, hoping to catch a glimpse of Josiah. She didn't know whether he was on a sloop or a brig fighting the Spanish at St George's Caye or whether he had joined his father with the troops at the other end of Haulover Creek. It was rumoured that Spanish forces were marching overland to destroy the settlement.

Leaving her shoes at the doorway to the house, Leah hurried indoors. She placed one finger against the pot, relieved that it was still piping hot. She enjoyed the smooth silkiness of the red Turkish carpet beneath her bare feet.

Two large gilded mirrors hung on opposite walls of the dining room. She caught glimpses of her face, half-hidden beneath the white headscarf, and of the fresh white apron covering her dress, which was made from coarse cotton that Leah had heard her mother call 'osnaburg'. It was the same fabric used for grain sacks, upholstery and, in tough times, curtains.

Listening to the murmur of voices on the verandah, she put the pot upon the silver tray which rested on the enormous sideboard. In her nervousness, Leah's hand bumped against a gleaming glass lamp. It wobbled but didn't fall against the numerous decanters of sherry and various wines crowding the surface of the sideboard. With a sigh of relief she walked across the polished pinewood floor, through the high, wide mahogany archway, into the commodious hall with beautiful pictures and mirrors. Occasional tables and comfortable chairs lined the walls. A brisk wind from the door leading to the verandah cooled her forehead. She carefully set down the tray on a serving table just outside the door.

Leah was helping her mother serve lunch to the two Angas brothers on the upstairs verandah of their three-storeyed white house which faced the sea.

The brothers liked to sit there, mornings and evenings, when they were not invited out, looking at the hustle and bustle of the trading vessels arriving and departing. Now they were looking through a telescope at the sloops, brigs, lighters and other boats guarding the northern passages and the mangrove islands called the Grand Bogue.

The brothers were merchants from Scotland and had lived in the settlement for a long time. They were known to be very rich, pious gentlemen who did all manner of good works for the poor, the slaves and the free, or for whoever approached them for help, as long as the brothers considered that they were deserving of assistance.

Mr Duncan Angas placed his telescope on the round table and sat facing the sea. He smoothed back his white hair, ruffled by the wind, and ran a bony finger around his collar. Sighing heavily he said, 'No boats from the battle in sight as yet today.'

'A miserable business. The Spaniards are going to get a taste of their own medicine this time, I'll be bound,' his brother, Mr Fife Angas, replied. He sat up straight, adjusted his stiff white jacket and picked up his coffee cup. 'A few more of the wounded arrived last night. The Baymen are holding their own, never fear, or we would have heard otherwise, surely.'

Mr Duncan Angas sighed again. 'At least three Baymen were killed and a few slaves. It disturbs me that we use the slaves to fight our battles.'

'Hiring them from Graham Lawson is bad enough. It troubles me but what else can we do?' Mr Fife Angas said. He helped himself to fried beef liver, onions and fresh bread, liberally buttered, from the plates Leah handed to him. 'The Almighty will surely forgive us, as you said.' He paused and added, 'I hope.'

'The good Lord has no reason to continue giving us his grace,' Mr Duncan replied. 'There is probably not a more immoral place under heaven than the settlement of Belize. We're only lucky all the slaves didn't desert us. In their place, who knows what I might have done.'

'You know better than to say such a thing, Duncan. You are a well-travelled man. Think of the wicked stories we've heard about Port Royal. I do agree that the Court House is no place for a Sunday service.' Mr Fife patted his lips with a large snowy napkin.

'The chaplain hurries the service so and before you can get a chance to speak with the fellow about anything, he's through the door and aboard his sailboat.' Mr Duncan tapped the side of his nose with irritation.

'That happened one or two times, as I recollect. A home-going vessel was waiting for his shipment of logwood and he needed to supervise his slaves,' Mr Fife said. He lifted the heavy silver pot and poured steaming coffee into a china cup. 'That's no example for the rest of the Baymen.'

'We need a proper place of worship, that's my view. Not that I can get any of the Baymen to help pay for it,' Mr Duncan said, rattling his fingernails against his cup.

'Come now, brother,' Mr Fife said, 'you are getting too excited.' He handed a handkerchief to Mr Duncan. 'Look at you, red as a beet and sweating to boot, with a fine breeze blowing.'

'I'd feel better if brother Ian was here. He knows a thing or two about battles at sea. We stand to lose everything if the Baymen lose this fight. We were outnumbered from the start.'

Leah remembered Mr Ian Angas, a tall, handsome sea captain who had been obliged to perform the burial service for a deceased settler because the chaplain had been so drunk he could not do his duty.

The arrival of Captain Ian Angas in the settlement was always a day of rejoicing for the brothers resident in Belize. Not only did the captain bring a variety of goods to sell in their large shop and letters from their relatives in Scotland and Jamaica but he also brought the latest books and newspapers from London, which they generously shared with their small circle of friends who met for bible readings almost every Sunday evening.

At those times, the brothers sat with their visitors at the large mahogany table in the dining room, their feet resting on the red, patterned Turkish carpet. Afterwards they retired to the parlour to sing hymns before drinking tea with sandwiches and cakes. Later in the evening the brothers and their guests discussed business and community affairs seated on comfortable, cushioned easy chairs on the cool verandah.

Often the books and papers were left open on tables and chairs in the parlour so that anyone curious about their contents could turn the pages without fear of detection. Especially interesting to Leah and her mother were those books and newspapers with cartoons and illustrations of strange places and foreign dress.

While the brothers talked, Leah stood against a far wall gazing out to sea, thinking about Will, who she knew for sure was behind the barricades set up on St Georges Caye, fighting alongside Mr Thomas McGilvrey. Something white was moving into her line of sight. Was it a sail?

As the fast messenger dorey drew nearer the shore, the crew

fired muskets and waved a white flag to signify that the Baymen had been victorious. The crowd on the foreshore let out a tremendous cheer. People clapped their hands and praised God, while others helped the exhausted men from the boats.

Leah heard the Angas brothers shouting, first one, then the other, then together, 'Hip, hip, hooray!'

'Let's drink to the Baymen,' Mr Duncan Angas said, raising his coffee cup and clinking it against his brother's. 'I knew they'd do it.'

The brothers stood at the verandah shouting and waving to the crowds below who were jumping up and down with excitement.

'Well done indeed,' Mr Fife Angas said. 'What a day! Very well done indeed, thanks be to God. We are saved.'

'To fight another day, I shouldn't wonder,' Mr Duncan Angas said. 'But thanks be to God for today.'

Leah watched the Baymen and slaves disembarking from several boats up and down the shore. Other boats bringing the sick and injured soon reached the shore and Leah heard a loud groan and cries from the crowd as three or more corpses, wrapped in sailcloth, were carried ashore.

Chapter 11

SEPTEMBER 1798
WILL

On the northeast end of the island, Will crouched on his haunches beside Sharper, peering from behind a breast-high barricade which they had helped to construct. It had been built over the last few days from beach sand backed by timber brought from the mainland. His Majesty's ship, the gun-brig *Merlin*, was taking up her position in emerald green water where she could manoeuvre more freely. A sailor stood in the crow's nest gesturing towards the approaching Spanish flotilla.

The brass fittings on the Merlin glinted in the sunlight and Will, his vision blurred, shook his head and rubbed his eyes, which burned from the brine on his hands.

The Baymen and their slaves, watchful and apprehensive, huddled in groups behind the barricades. Above their muted voices and restive movements, Will heard the soughing of scorched coconut trees, the hissing of the waves and the clank of swords.

Every now and then he caught a whiff of the acrid scent from charred and burnt houses. The sour smell combined with the pungent odour of sweating, stinking, anxious men made him want to retch.

'Not sick, are you?' Sharper asked, brushing sand off his musket.

'I'm feeling all right,' Will said, shoving his pistol into his waistband. 'My eyesight must be getting bad, though.'

'Your eyesight? That's sudden. You were spotting mahogany trees last season.'

'Sudden or not,' Will said, 'you have a look and tell me if you see black fellows on the *Merlin*.'

Sharper lifted his head and peered over the barricade. He

73

sucked in his breath. 'You're right,' he said, 'black troops for sure, or so they look like to me.'

'Slaves like us, do you think?' Will asked, running a tentative finger along his machete, as though testing the keenness of the blade.

Sharper shook his head doubtfully. 'I think they must be free, don't you?'

'Or on their way to being free,' Will said, 'lucky them. Maybe we could get to Jamaica and join those troops.'

'You and your big ideas,' Sharper said, keeping his eyes on the *Merlin*. 'I think they must have more than a hundred men on that ship.'

'The Baymen, with us slaves, have – what – four or five hundred?'

'Something like that,' Sharper said. 'A spy told my friend that the Spanish have many more hundreds. We'll beat them in any case. We know these waters. It's a wonder the reef didn't wreck a ship or two.'

'No chance of that now,' Will said. He sighed, stretching out his legs, which were cramped. The afternoon was hot and humid and his skin felt clammy; he longed for a bucket of rain water to rinse the salt from his skin.

Sharper was saying, 'Things look bad right now but with the King's ship behind us we can't lose. It's a pity the Jamaican Governor only sent the one ship but there's bound to be more on the way.'

'No doubt,' Will said. He had not been infected by the martial spirit which Sharper, the other slaves and their masters were feeling so passionately. Will would have preferred to be fighting against the British settlers rather than helping them repel the Spaniards from the settlement of Belize.

He felt out of place and knew that the settlers expected many of the slaves to desert. Spies and emissaries of the Spanish had offered them their masters' houses, property and money if they would rise up and help them defeat the British.

Will thought about the two Spanish spies in Belize Town who had been caught, tried and hung outside the prison before sunset on the same day. He closed his eyes against the image of the men swinging on the gibbet. He tried to listen to Sharper, who was naming the Baymen vessels defending the northern approach. 'That's the *Tickler*, then the *Towser* and the *Swinger*, all shallow water boats to my mind.'

Will took a pint of coconut oil from Sharper's canvas bag. He rubbed the oil all over his body to soothe the fiercely itching insect bites. During the previous night the wind had dropped for a few hours and the sand-flies had been almost unbearable.

As he re-corked the bottle with a bit of coconut husk, he began to accept the fact that if he was going to save his life, it was vital that he show enthusiasm for this fight. The failure of the small slave uprising a few months before still filled him with dread not only for himself but for Sharper and their comrades. There had been no hint yet that anyone knew that he and Sharper had been the ringleaders but the fear of being betrayed was with them all the time. They were always watching their step, speaking guardedly with others, feeling relatively free only when they were sent out on mahogany spotting expeditions.

'Over there,' Sharper was saying, his voice almost hoarse with excitement, 'there's the *Teazer*, and the *Mermaid*.'

'Yes,' Will said, resting his head against the barricade and closing his eyes. The sun had gone behind the clouds, the wind was blowing harder and the waves were getting choppy. The noise of the sea, the flapping of canvas, the clinking of machetes and swords and the rising voices of over a hundred men made Will's heart beat faster. He swallowed the lump in his throat, unwilling to believe that he was feeling such acute anxiety. The stiffening sea breezes seemed to be stopping his breath.

He heard the roar of voices subside to a murmur. He sat up

as Sharper gripped his arm. Looking over the barricade, they saw three Spanish brigs and a dozen schooners bearing down on the caye. The slaves, with their owners in formation behind them, took up their positions as the Spaniards drew closer and closer to the guarded channel.

If the Baymen were defeated, the sea-lanes would be open for the Spanish ships to sail to Belize Town where the townspeople waited in agonized suspense for news of the outcome of this battle. Their lives and the livelihood of the British settlers depended on victory.

'Very heavy metal,' Will said. 'The guns look like eighteen-pounders, maybe even bigger. What have we got?'

'The *Merlin*'s cannons look to me like twelve and sixteen. The Baymen have maybe an eighteen. The others are nine- and six-pounders, maybe.'

As the Spanish ships sailed nearer, their troops opened fire but they were still too far away and their shots fell short. Not much damage was done ashore, where the Baymen and their slaves waited grimly for the signal to attack. It did not come.

There had been several skirmishes during the past few days with the Spanish near other cayes along the coast. At first there had been hope that the Spanish would consider themselves beaten and retreat back to Campeche and the Rio Hondo but their courage and determination seemed undaunted.

'You'll fight, won't you Will?' Sharper asked. 'I mean you won't go over? You can now, you know.'

'I'm not going over,' Will said, thinking of Sharper's friendship and his unswerving loyalty over the years. Trying to keep his voice steady, Will said, 'I'll fight.'

'Then they'll call us loyal and patriotic, you see, Will. I'm thinking of my children, you know?'

'They'll count us as brave, eh?' Will asked. 'The white man, the black man, the master, the slave?'

'Why do you have to make a pappyshow out of everything, Will? You understand very well what I mean.'

Will touched Sharper's arms briefly, reassuringly, and felt his friend's muscles quivering. 'I do understand,' Will said, thinking of Leah and wondering if they'd ever have a family together.

'You'll give as good as you get?' Sharper asked, his broad face paling almost to the colour of ashes.

'No flinching and no quailing by me,' Will said, watching Sharper's dark eyes brighten with hope.

'Then we'll win,' he said. 'The other guys will catch our spirit if we are together.'

'We're together,' Will said, feeling his throat constrict. He meant what he'd said but he would be fighting against the grain, giving up the possibility of the freedom he'd struggled for from the moment that he and his mother had been captured and enslaved. He wondered what she would say if she could see him now. He couldn't bear to think that she was dead or that he would never see her again.

'They're getting closer,' Sharper said, his face grim, 'and still no signal to fire.'

'Waiting for the captain of the *Merlin*, I expect,' Will said. 'Let's see if we can figure out the plan.'

Will and Sharper fixed their attention on the Spanish flag-ship and five gun-brigs which continued to bear down on the caye.

'Bad move,' Sharper said, spitting onto the sand.

'They'll beach themselves on the shoals.'

'Let's hope you're right,' Will said, getting a closer look at the Spanish ships loaded with heavy guns and hundreds of men firing at the caye with little effect. 'Still no signal yet.'

'That may be the plan. On the shoals and then hand to hand,' Sharper said, tightening the string around his trousers. 'Look sharp, Will. This could be it.'

Chapter 12

Will was almost relieved that the fight, sure to be bloody, would soon be over one way or another. It had been a long week without definite news about the Spanish forces marching by land towards Belize Town. He wondered how Leah would fare if the Spanish ravaged the town as they'd done in the past. Would she, Hannah and Sam join them and escape to the promised freedom? If their lives were spared, what other choice would they have?

Around them on the island, every man was in position and silent, their eyes fixed on the approaching ships. He picked out Thomas McGilvrey, his curly brown hair pulled back and tied with a black ribbon. To his right was Graham Lawson's son, Marshall, a red bandana around his throat, his hair in a plait which hung down to his waist. They wore white shirts with long full sleeves and tight black breeches shoved into high black boots, stained with dirt and sea water. McGilvrey and Lawson each held a sword in one hand and a pistol in the other.

Will grasped Congo Jack's yoke-wood. Other slaves were armed with pistols and machetes and pokonoboy sticks covered with thorns. The white settlers called the slave fighters carrying sticks the 'poke-and-doh' boys because of the imported salted pork and flour rations distributed to them when they paddled upriver by pit-pans. The mahogany banks were often one hundred to two hundred miles upriver.

Will had cringed when Marshall Lawson had called out to him earlier that day, 'You there, poke-and-doh boy, bring that tar-pail over this way.' Will had taken his time before obeying, which had caused Lawson to swear at him, his voice ringing out across the caye.

Will nearly said, 'My mother's home-name for me was Nzimbu which means valuable shell.' He didn't, of course. Although the images from his boyhood were becoming less clear now, less real, those memories helped to sustain him in his exile. He did not intend to have them sullied, especially by bat-eared Marshall Lawson. The strength necessary to control his temper had flayed his insides with as much viciousness as the knotted cat-o'-nine-tails with which he'd been beaten several times in the settlement. He'd covered his face with his hands and said to himself, 'Oh mother, oh Leah.' The names had served as a temporary balm to his wounded spirits.

Will now regretted that he had allowed Congo Jack's opinion to influence his decision not to see Leah before he had left. His feet were near to the sea and he listened and watched for the signal to fight. He glanced at a school of long-guards, like tiny, skinny lizards, darting back and forth through the seaweed in the crystal clear water. He thought of Leah again. She loved the sea, perhaps because, like Sharper, she had been born in the settlement, while he still felt like a foreigner and was still treated like one.

Compared to the vast forests where he served out his time, St George's Caye seemed so small to Will and so open to the vast sea. The sea was almost white nearest the shore, emerald green farther out and a deep blue where it foamed over the barrier reef. He'd begun to hate the incessant sounds of tumbling waves and the stiff breezes which blew the acrid scent of the seventeen burnt houses across his face. His lips felt dry and cracked and he was shivering – whether from the fear of death, fever or both, it was difficult for him to tell. He fingered his flask, tempted to take a sip of water, but decided to wait a while longer. Who knew when fresh water would be distributed again?

As the Spanish ships sailed into the channel one after another, shouts of triumph from the settlers and their slaves rang through the air.

'Hard and fast,' Sharper said, 'they're beached on the sand. I knew that would happen. It's too shallow there for those ships. What a bram-bram, what a bump-and-bore,' he added as he stared at the confusion of the soldiers on the listing ships.

'Too late to tow off now,' Will said, watching the flagship and the three following vessels in a fix on the sandy shoals.

The men raised a rallying cry as the signal for battle was hoisted. The Baymen started firing canisters packed with shot at the Spanish ships which were now in close range. Will was staring mesmerized when a magazine of ammunition exploded on a Spanish schooner, killing and maiming many of the men on board. The ship was in flames and the Spanish troops were in dreadful confusion as they tried to escape from the blazing vessel.

'The other ships are trying to get away,' Sharper shouted to Will. 'They're fouling one another, ship and ship.'

'Six are getting away,' Will said, watching the Spanish get safely into open water while firing broadsides at the *Merlin* and the Baymen vessels guarding the channel. The air was filled with the smell of gunpowder and the sky seemed to have darkened as the settlers on caye loaded and re-loaded their guns, pouring shot onto the Spanish ships grounded on the shoals. The volleys of musket fire came swift and fast.

Above them squawking seagulls and black frigate birds flew high above the fray. Brown pelicans abandoned their posts, their huge wings flapping as they made for safer perches far away.

'McGilvrey and Lawson are giving us the signal to board,' Sharper said. 'Look sharp, Will. Stop staring and move or they'll shoot you or run you down.'

'All right, all right,' Will said. 'Let's get to the boats.'

'Two pit-pans to every Spanish ship, that's the order,' McGilvrey said to Will and Sharper. 'You two are in this one with Lawson and myself.'

'Board where you can,' Lawson was shouting. 'Board where you can. Dig in your paddles, men.'

As he listened to Marshall Lawson firing orders left and right, Will wondered how much he knew of his father's declining fortunes. Did he know that he was planning to settle his gambling debts by signing away his mahogany banks to Thomas McGilvrey? Will doubted it or he would not be fighting alongside McGilvrey.

Will and Sharper moved to the bow of the boat, joining the other slaves who paddled swiftly towards the Spanish ships. The large desperate crews were frantically trying to shove their four ships off the shoals. The Baymen and their slaves on the gun-flats and droghers to the rear of the Spanish ships released volleys of musket fire as the men in the pit-pans tried to board the ships, fiercely battling with the Spaniards in an attempt to clear the bulwarks.

Wild musketry fire met them as they paddled alongside the Spanish ship. As Will and Sharper clambered hand over fist, fighting their way up to the deck, three slaves were shot. Will grappled with a Spanish soldier, throwing him overboard. All around him wounded and dying men were falling to the deck and into the sea. As he fought on, he felt like his terrified younger self aboard the slaving ship to the West Indies from Africa. He had watched the crew throw sick and dying slaves overboard. He would never forget their anguished cries and the slender hands of a woman, about his mother's age, trying to grab at the side of the sailing ship.

The desperate Spaniards fought with might and main to hold back the settlers and slaves. Will and Sharper, braces of pistols in their waistbands, struggled to gain footholds on the deck, which was slippery with blood. The Baymen and slaves advanced foot by foot, machetes raised and pistols firing.

Sharper shot wide at a Spanish soldier rushing towards them. The Spaniard thrust a bayonet into Sharper's left arm, which held a raised machete. Will knocked the bayonet out of the Spaniard's hand with Congo Jack's yoke-wood and struck the Spaniard's skull with his machete. He helped Sharper, who was screaming with pain, to quickly remove the bayonet blade. His blood spattered onto the dead Spaniard's long, matted black hair.

Dazed with pain, Sharper shrugged off Will's arm and side by side, with other Baymen and slaves, they continued pushing back the Spaniards until they began falling or jumping overboard. Amidst the noise of pistol shot and the clang of machetes and swords, Will heard McGilvrey shouting his name.

Will heard him call again and again but beside him Sharper's arm was bleeding profusely and he appeared about to faint. To Will time seemed to have stopped as he fended off their attackers. Sharper was still firing at the Spaniards when he stumbled across a dead body and fell head foremost onto the main mast. Blood spurted from his forehead and Will, dragging him by his good arm, kept firing as he made his way towards McGilvrey, who was standing over Marshall Lawson. Lawson lay dead on the deck. His grey eyes were wide open and Will, leaning down, closed them quickly.

'Good God,' McGilvrey was saying, 'where were you two? You were supposed to watch our backs. Don't let Lawson be thrown overboard. Fend off all comers from this end.'

Will, pistol in hand, pushed back the bodies of two dead Spaniards and said to Sharper, 'Lie down, lie down. Try not to move – pretend you're dead.'

Sharper slumped over, groaning with pain, and Will stood against the ship's railing guarding them both. He picked up Lawson's sword and removed his pistols.

At the other end of the ship he saw McGilvrey in the thick of the settlers who were cutting down the last of the Spanish soldiers. The Spanish commander was still battling bravely alongsise his remaining men. But he was now outnumbered and as he raised his sword, a settler shot him through the heart and he fell down dead across the bodies of his defeated men.

Shouting with triumph, the settlers and slaves rushed the remaining soldiers, who threw down their arms, leaped overboard or cried for mercy.

Will knelt by Sharper and said to him, 'We've won, Sharper. You were right, we won.' Will bandaged Sharper's arm and forehead with strips from a torn shirt he had removed from a dead slave. Sharper groaned, opened his eyes briefly, but did not reply.

Leaning against the railing, Will watched the *Merlin* and the Baymen vessels pouring shot into the Spanish ships, which were forced to line up in the narrow channel. The Spanish ships were wrecked, foremasts down, with the dead and dying littering the decks. Unable to withstand the raking fire of case shot from the *Merlin*, one by one the Spanish ships hauled their sails and made for Long Caye and Caye Chapel where they would bury their dead. Two disabled schooners were left behind and the crew of the *Merlin* captured them with no further resistance.

Chapter 13

As the exhausted slaves, some of them wounded, paddled away from St George's Caye towards Belize Town, Will said to Sharper, 'We'll soon get back. How are you holding up?' He adjusted the blood-soaked bandage around Sharper's arm.

'As good as you, I expect,' Sharper said. 'You've a nasty cut on your forehead. The sea water will keep down the infection. Are you hurt anywhere else?'

'A few cuts and bruises here and there – nothing much. We were lucky.'

'Yes,' Sharper said, looking towards another pit-pan travelling a little ahead of them.

'Lawson's body is in that boat along with one or two others,' Will said.

McGilvrey sat in the stern of the boat, his head in his hands, his hair blowing about his face, his shirt torn to ribbons and one arm bandaged. Will wondered how McGilvrey would tell Graham Lawson about the death of his son. In his experience there was no right or easy way to deliver a message of death, especially the death of a family member.

'The wounded are to go to the Court House,' Will said to Sharper. 'McGilvrey and some of the settlers' slaves will get Lawson's body to his father's compound.'

'They'll send for Hannah, I expect,' Sharper said.

'There's nobody like her at a time like this. McGilvrey told me to find her as soon as we're through at the Court House.'

Will felt buoyed up by McGilvrey's orders to find Hannah and Leah; they were to leave whatever they were doing to help with the preparations for Lawson's funeral.

'What's to happen at the Court House?' Sharper asked. He stared at the roughening waves leaping up and then falling back again.

'A surgeon's mate is treating some of the wounded there.' A wave splashed over the side of the boat, drenching them with water. It was almost night when they spied the rooftops of the town which lay below the level of the sea.

Dozens of boats were already in the harbour. The passengers disembarked near the Foreshore and stumbled towards the Court House, a one-storey building roofed with thatch and raised on posts about eight feet off the ground. Will and Sharper lined up with other slaves on the muddy ground underneath the Court House. Some slaves, too badly injured, lay on the ground around them. They were tended by female relatives and other slaves who were expert in using healing herbs, tree barks and salves.

As they waited their turn, Will and Sharper observed the wounded settlers as they were carried, some on litters, up the Court House steps to the verandah where the chaplain rang the bell for church services on Sundays. The Court House could hold about two hundred people. Inside were cushioned mahogany chairs and large tables for the magistrates, a jury box, a witness box and a dock made from carved mahogany where accused prisoners stood.

After their wounds were attended to by the female slaves and bandaged by the surgeon's mate, Will and Sharper made their way to Graham Lawson's compound.

Sharper still felt weak and so they walked slowly, talking about the battle with the Spanish and the dead slaves and settlers they had known.

As they neared the compound, Will looked down the side-lane but there was no oil lamp burning near the closed shop where Congo Jack usually sat. He'd probably gone upriver as he'd said he would. Congo Jack's yoke-wood had been left lying among the dead bodies on the Spanish ship. Will didn't think he would mind. By now he'd probably have found himself a new one.

Lamp lights burned in every room in Graham Lawson's house and they heard voices on the verandah and in the living room. Will wondered if Thomas McGilvrey was there, describing to Graham Lawson and the visiting settlers how bravely Marshall Lawson had fought and died at the battle of St George's Caye.

As they passed the kitchen, situated away from the main house, they saw Miss Quasheba, the cook, and her helper, Berry, preparing dinner.

'A happy return,' she called from the window. 'On your feet I see, praises be. No worse for wear, I hope?' She pushed her plump face, upper body and arms through the window to observe them more closely.

'Shaper's arm is quite bad Miss Sheba, but he was attended to at the Court House,' Will said. 'The bandage on my head looks worse than my cut.'

'Very glad to hear it,' Miss Sheba said, her kind face brightening. 'I made a nice big pot of fish stew and baked fresh Creole bread. Berry here will bring food out to you in a few minutes.'

Berry, a tall, skinny girl, peered around Miss Sheba's shoulders to get a better look at the two men. She gave a sharp squeal as she saw the blood on Will's bandage and Sharper's arm in a sling.

'Get back to your work, girl,' Miss Sheba said. 'That Berry is more a hindrance than a help.' She called over her shoulder, 'Where are you going now, Berry? Stay right there and watch the fire-hearth. I don't want that stew to burn.'

'Visitors upstairs already, I see. Everybody hungry and thirsty I expect, Miss Sheba?' asked Will.

'Yes, yes, indeed. It is a sad day for Master Lawson but Master Marshall killed a few of the Spanish I hear.'

'That he did, mam,' Sharper replied, leaning heavily against Will.

'Well, we'll give him a fine farewell, for his poor mother's sake. She was a good lady. At her last she said to me, "Quasheba" –

that's what she always called me – "Quasheba," she said to me, "even in life we are in death."'

Miss Sheba wiped her eyes with the corner of her apron. 'I helped to raise Master Marshall before he went to school. Such a change in him this last time he returned. His mother will be glad to see him again.'

'Sorry for your sorrow, Miss Sheba,' Will said. 'Sharper and I will go in now, if you don't mind.'

'Go in, get some rest,' Miss Sheba said. 'I hope you gave as good as you got, Sharper?'

'So I did, mam. So we both did.'

'Not surprised at all,' Miss Sheba said in a regretful tone, as though she wanted to talk with them some more. As they moved off, she said, 'Will, please remember to tell Hannah and Leah to bring Sam with them, if he's not hauling and carrying elsewhere. I'll need him for running up and down the stairs.'

'I'll do that, mam,' Will said, 'and thank you.'

Will lit the hurricane lantern and placed it near the door of their room to the rear of the compound. He unrolled a mat on the hard-packed earth and helped Sharper to situate himself as comfortably as possible, putting rolled clothing under his head and giving him some water to drink. He then lit the hurricane lamp, placing it near the door.

Outside the room, Will drank as much water as he could hold and poured calabash after calabash of water over his body, careful to keep his bandaged head dry. The water made his cuts and bruises sting. His whole body felt as if it had been hit by a falling mahogany tree.

He heard Sharper call his name, his voice anxious.

'Do you want some more water?' Will asked. 'Berry will bring out the food in a minute.'

'Aren't you hungry?' Sharper asked. 'Wait and have some with me.'

'I'll have mine later,' Will said. 'I'd better get to the Angas house to see if they are still there. If not, I'll go to Overpond – that's where their rooms are.'

'Don't stay too long and overdo things, Will. When are you going to sleep?'

'I don't feel tired,' Will said. 'Don't wait up for me.'

As he stepped outside the compound he looked at the spot where, only a few days before, Marshall Lawson had sat with his paints, newspapers and books. He looked up at the stars, which looked like brilliant sparks in the night sky. He gave thanks that he had made it safely back.

Chapter 14

Will walked for about fifty yards along the Foreshore to the home of the Angas brothers but Leah and Hannah had already left for the day. He continued through the dark alleys and streets until he reached the swampy back roads of Overpond. The swamp was partially filled in with wood chips, rum bottles, conch shells and other debris to create drier ground. Most of the poor black people and slaves lived close to the great swamps, some distance away from the sea.

He walked until he reached the numerous yards flanked with long rows of what people called 'negro houses'. They were really like separate rooms under one long roof. The beating of the goombay drums in a nearby yard made his injured head throb. To him they did not speak of victory but of those slaves who had died in the fighting during the past six or seven days. St George's Caye was an island Will hoped never to see again as long as he lived. He suspected that the ghosts of the dead slaves would join the other phantoms from his old world to inhabit his dreams during the nights to come, from which he would awake shaking with terror and drenched in sweat.

'Evening to you, Mother Cap,' he said to an old woman frying grated coconut meat in an iron pot over a huge open fire. She fanned the smoke from her eyes, which were sunk into her wrinkled face. The smoke caused tears to stream down her cheeks and her toothless gums made her mouth seem mashed in.

Using a long-handled spoon to skim the oil from the brown coconut trash, she said, 'Evening to you, Will.' She pointed with her spoon at his bandaged head. 'Glad to see you safe again. It's a sad day for some.'

'Yes, Mother, a sad day for some,' Will said. There was a hump as large as a pineapple on her shoulders, her hands were gnarled and the joints swollen.

As he continued on his way, Will wondered why he had been so moved tonight by the old slave woman. Old women like Mother Cap, who made their living in the best way they could, were an ordinary sight in the streets of the town. Perhaps it was because she reminded him that wherever there were slaves in the world, his mother could be facing the same fate.

When he reached the room where Hannah, Leah and Sam lived, Will saw them hanging their washing out to dry on the branches and bushes growing in the nearby swamp.

'Hello Leah, Hannah, Sam.' He was surprised at the joy in his heart. He opened his arms as they came running to him.

'Happy return, Will. Will is alive. Happy return,' Leah said.

He hugged the three of them, feeling the hot tears rolling down his unshaven cheeks.

They went to sit on the steps to their room and as Will told them about the battle, he felt Sam's hand steal into his own.

Will picked up a handful of woodchips that Leah and Sam had spread all over the swampy area in front of their room. He moved the chips backwards and forwards in his hands. Then he said, 'Marshall Lawson was killed on the Spanish ship.'

'So that's why you're here,' Leah said. 'They need Mama, isn't that right Will?'

'They do,' Will said. 'McGilvrey wants both you and Hannah and Sam.'

'McGilvrey sent for us?' Hannah asked.

'Yes, Mam,' Will said. 'He's in charge at the moment. Mr Lawson is not up to much, of course.'

'I heard he'd not been keeping at all well, even before this happened. Is McGilvrey in charge of all of us too?' Hannah asked.

'I don't know for sure if Mr Lawson is ill, other than I've heard him coughing now and then. But McGilvrey is giving the marching orders now – at least until after the funeral.'

Leah sighed. 'We'd better get ready Mama.'

Will looked at Hannah, who was holding one hand over her eyes as though she did not want them to see her face. She rose to her feet and said, 'We won't be long Will, if you can wait for us.' She placed a gentle hand on Will's bandaged forehead. 'Your eyes were spared, which is a blessing.'

'I can wait,' Will said, 'I've had worse injuries in the bush.'

'I know that well enough,' Hannah said. 'Leah and Sam, come and give me a hand. We'll be over there for about two days at least.'

In a few minutes, they were ready to go with Will to Graham Lawson's compound. Will shouldered a number of rolled mats and bundles of clothing. He followed with Leah behind Hannah and Sam. Around them, cattlemen, huntsmen, axemen and a variety of forest workers were preparing to leave for the mahogany camps up and down the river.

'When are you and Sharper going back upriver, Will?' Leah asked, shifting her bundle from one hand to the other.

'As soon as the funeral is over,' Will replied. 'In a day or two. I was hoping to get a chance to talk with you.' He felt as though everything in his future life depended on these few minutes with Leah.

'It's a pity you can't stay longer,' Leah said, 'at least until you feel a bit better.' She laid a hand on his arm. 'It was a really fretful time while you were gone.'

'I was worried about you too and Hannah and Sam,' Will said, biting his lower lip. Leah had not seemed to want his company during the two weeks he'd been in town before he'd sailed to St George's Caye.

He'd gone to those places where he thought it likely she would be. Once or twice he'd caught glimpses of her holding hands with Josiah Potts on the Foreshore, or sitting on the grass at the Barracks near the Clare sisters' house.

'Do you ever think of those days upriver, Leah?'

'Yes,' Leah said, lowering her eyelids, which seemed swollen, as though she'd been crying at some point during the day. She kept biting her lips to keep them from trembling.

'Do you remember what I asked you?' Will asked, recalling Congo Jack's words of advice and wondering if he had been wrong to warn him against talking with Leah.

Leah hung her head to one side but she did not reply.

He looked down at Leah holding a bundle in the crook of her arm. She'd lost weight and her face had lost its roundness and its glow. She looked disconsolate and he missed the easy, confiding way they'd spoken to each other during the time she'd spent upriver.

'I'm asking you again, Leah, in spite of...'

'In spite of what?' Leah asked. Her eyes were startled, her face angry, as she looked up at him.

'I think you have a sweetheart now, so things are different. But I love you Leah and, if you agree, I'll try to get us our freedom. Would you marry me then?'

'Why are you saying these things, Will? What do you know about my life here?'

'Not much, Leah, but I think you are putting your hopes in the wrong person.'

'If you are talking about Josiah, you are wrong,' she said, hurrying ahead to catch up with Hannah and Sam.

'Leah, wait a bit,' Will said, hastening his steps until he was walking beside her again. 'Listen, if things don't go right for you, will you send me a message?'

Leah was crying now, rubbing her face on the bundle she carried. 'I like you very much, Will, but I can't be your sweetheart and I couldn't be your wife, even if you managed to free us both. Try to understand.'

'I won't ever say anything again, Leah. I don't want to make you unhappy. You don't hate me, do you?'

'Oh, no, Will,' she said, standing up to kiss him on the cheek, 'you are my best friend.'

'And you are mine, Leah,' Will said, wishing he could protect her, but he was powerless to do more than he had tried to do. He put a hand to the bandage on his aching head.

After they had walked a little way, they reached the large, elegant homes on the sea front. The lanes leading to the Foreshore were already crowded with slaves making their way to the Lawson compound; they would spend the night here at the wake for Marshall Lawson. Will heard the distant beat of the goombay drums, female voices raised in conversation and song and the furious barking of the dogs penned up beneath the house. The gates were wide open to anyone who wanted to enter the yard.

As Will followed Hannah, Leah and Sam, Miss Sheba looked through the window and called, 'Hannah, you're here. Come right up. We've made everything ready for you in Master Marshall's room.'

Chapter 15

LEAH

Leah hurried through the crowded compound to the rear of the Lawson house. Slaves were gathered in groups in the yard, in the lane, near the huts and underneath the verandah in front of the barred doors of the shop. There was no moon but the sky was full of stars. The wind from the sea swooshed through the towering trees, threatening to extinguish the lamps and candles in the huts.

Sharper was lying in one of the huts. She hoped that he wasn't in too much pain. The wake, with drumming, singing and dancing, would last until morning when the coffin would be carried on the shoulders of slaves to the burial ground.

The thought of her mother preparing Marshall Lawson for burial in his best clothes made Leah's stomach queasy. It must be awful for Hannah to be in the same house as Graham Lawson, who had not wanted to have anything to do with any of them for as long as Leah could remember. Whatever the relationship had been between Graham Lawson and her mother, it could not have been a pleasant one. The talk with Will had also left her feeling downhearted. She didn't like to hurt Will but she couldn't imagine what else she could have said.

Her spirits lifted a little when she saw Sukie in the middle of a group of women, preparing food on a fire-hearth at the far end of the compound. The slaves were filling the yard almost to overflowing. Leah called out to her but Sukie, on seeing Leah, turned away in an unfriendly fashion.

'Did you just cut your eye at me?' Leah asked, trying to make a joke of Sukie's snub. Leah had to raise her voice above the loud conversation and laughter, the pounding of drums and the incessant rattling of sheck'as, gourds and coconut shells containing seeds of various kinds. She began helping Sukie to arrange glasses of spiced wine on one tray and cups of ginger tea on the other.

'You can just stop moving those glasses and cups around, Miss Leah,' Sukie said, throwing back her soft, silky hair. 'Miss Quasheba says that you are to serve the visitors upstairs.'

'Let me stay here then and you can go up, if you like,' Leah said, hoping to see Sukie's scowl relax, but Sukie turned back to rearranging the tray.

'It's all right,' she said, 'it's not your fault that I'm not wanted upstairs. It's because I am black and my nose is flat.'

'Aie, Sukie, don't keep saying things like that,' Leah said, pouring coffee into cups and bowls of every description, probably borrowed from other slave compounds.

'It's true, Leah. And you know I'm not really a slave at all and shouldn't be treated like one.' She looked at Leah, her dark eyes gleaming with malice. 'No offence to you, Leah.'

'I'd better go and see Miss Quasheba,' Leah said, anxious to get away from Sukie's indignant face.

'Anybody with eyes can look at me and see that I'm obviously Miskito, not from around here.' She waved a plump arm dismissively, which Leah understood to mean the entire settlement.

'Where are you from then?' Leah asked, just to be provocative, for Sukie had told her this story before. 'You were born here.'

'Yes but my mother was from the Miskito Shore, leastways I think that's what people tell me.'

'Oh, those Indians that come here sometimes? Why would you want to be like them?' To Leah, the Indians that regularly visited the settlement from the Miskito Shore looked as badly off as Sukie and herself.

'Because then I'd be free, that's why.' She looked wistful, pressing her lips together so that the dimples showed in her cheeks.

'But you don't look like a brown-skinned Indian, Sukie,' Leah said.

'You know I have African blood, Leah, no need to remind me. But I am mostly Indian and other things so I should be free.' She glanced up at the open windows of the Lawson house, muttering under her breath. 'That's our half-brother lying dead up there, not that it means anything to anybody.'

She looked sad. Leah relented, saying the words she knew Sukie needed to hear. 'We might prove it one of these days,' she said.

'I know I can prove it if I ever get the chance,' Sukie said, jutting out her chin. The determination on Sukie's face was almost comical but Leah did not laugh.

'You wouldn't be any better off than you are now, surely?' Leah asked, trying to look as though this was only common sense after all.

'That's all you know about it, Leah,' she said, picking up the jugs of wine as people began lining up in front of the trestle tables. Then she added, 'And that's less than little.'

They both laughed as they poured drinks into cups and passed them to people. 'Another time you'll have to tell me the story again, if you like.'

Leah knew Sukie's story off by heart, for it was similar to stories she'd heard about other slaves in the settlement. Many of them had been forced to leave the Miskito Shore and brought as slaves to the settlement at Belize which, according to rumour, was against British law.

'Oh, by the way,' Sukie said, as Leah was moving off towards the kitchen stairs, 'that Master Potts gave me this to give you.' She removed an envelope from her apron pocket and handed it to Leah.

'When?' Leah asked, wondering why Sukie had not mentioned it earlier.

'He was in the shop to buy cough medicine for his mother,

96

that's what he said anyway, so Master Dickey went to the back to make it up specially for him. I was sweeping the floor at the time.'

Leah looked at Sukie, who shamefacedly said, 'In the confusion here I forgot all about it, to tell you the truth.'

Graham Lawson rented Sukie to Master Dickey, the apothecary, and his Creole mistress. Sukie had told Leah that as horrible a household as it was, she valued her place there, for she had narrowly escaped being put in a yard with a group of women who were whispered about in the town. 'Breeders, people call them,' Sukie had said. 'But don't tell anyone, Leah, promise?'

With the memory of that conversation in mind, Leah said, 'That's all right.'

'Master Potts and his family are still up there waiting to view the body.' She looked Leah up and down. 'You'd better watch your step. I've been hearing gossip.'

'What kind?' Leah asked, her fingers trembling as she placed the envelope inside the bosom of her dress.

'You'll find out soon enough,' Sukie said. 'I don't repeat gossip, as you well know.'

Chapter 16

As Leah climbed the stairs to the kitchen, her heart was racing and she felt slightly breathless. She set down her bundle near her feet and read the short message: *'Try to get away. I'll be on the Foreshore at ten o'clock for about one hour.'* The note further unsettled Leah for Josiah usually met her after work outside the Clares' house, on the nearby road, or by some other seemingly random chance. Why had Josiah given the note to Sukie, in the apothecary's shop, thus making their relationship so plain?

She looked over the railing at the African slaves gathered in their various nations and the Creole slaves in their own groups. People were playing cards, backgammon or dice.

Near the huts, she noticed Will dancing in a circle of people. He'd stuck a grey and white fowl feather in the bandage around his head, his eyes were closed, his body naked to the waist and he wore tight black pants which stopped below his knees. His bare feet were moving across the ground as though he was flying, his arms spread wide, one arm slightly higher than the other like a bird wheeling in the air. Will seemed to float over the ground as though he was in a trance. High above the beating drums, she heard the wail of a flute and the jingling of tiny bells around Will's ankle.

'Ah, Will,' Leah said to herself, feeling her heart move within her. She wanted to rush downstairs to comfort him, to tell him how sorry she was, how much she understood, but she could not say the words that would make him feel like himself again.

She moved away from the railing, entered the kitchen, hung her bundle on a hook behind the door and joined the group of slaves lining up to receive laden trays from the cook. Leah smelt beef roasting on a spit and saw pastries and bread laid out on a cooling rack. There was a rattling of cutlery and a clatter of serving dishes. Miss Sheba and two older assistants were giving instructions to women like Leah who were carrying food into the house.

'Ah, here you are Leah,' Miss Sheba said. 'These plates are ready, take them in and please don't break anything.'

Leah re-crossed the bridge to the main house, pushed open the green baize door to the dining room and walked over to deposit the dinner plates on the sideboard. As she collected the used glasses, cups and saucers she saw Josiah, dressed in a full black suit and white shirt, his beard neatly trimmed. He stood leaning against the wall, drinking a glass of red wine. He crossed the floor to her and placed his empty glass on her tray.

'Did you get the note?' he asked. 'Is the time all right?' His speech was slurred and he swayed a little.

'Yes,' Leah said, moving along to collect glasses left on tables in the large room and on the verandah. She glanced towards the stairs to the bedroom, wondering when Hannah would be finished. Before she met Josiah she had to prepare pans of hot water on the downstairs fire-hearth for her mother's bath.

A space for the coffin had been cleared in the middle of the room and people were seated against the walls. She noticed Thomas McGilvrey talking with the Angas brothers, and the Clare sisters. She saw other people whom she recognized. Sitting with Josiah's parents were various merchants, magistrates and other slaveholders. Graham Lawson was seated on the verandah with the chaplain, the Reverend Matthew Burke. Cigar smoke floated about the room. One of the magistrates was softly playing hymns on the piano in an adjoining room. Some of the women had their perfumed silk handkerchiefs in their hands, pressing them every now and then to their eyes.

As she approached the Angas brothers to collect their glasses, she heard Mr Fife Angas say, 'Lovely tune that. *Amazing Grace*, I think it's called. Heard it for the first time when our brother, Ian, was here last.'

'I like it myself,' Thomas McGilvrey was saying. 'I believe it was written by a reformed captain of a slave ship, the Reverend

John Newton.'

'Is that right? I hadn't heard,' Mr Fife Angas said. 'Ah, here you are Leah, just in time. I was wondering what to do with my glass.'

Leah looked up to see Thomas McGilvrey holding out his glass expectantly, so she proffered the tray and he said, 'Well, well. And how are you, Miss Leah? Have you and your brother been fishing lately?'

'Not yet, sir. We hope to go again before the mauger season ends.'

'Those oysters were just the thing. If you get any more, please tell cook.'

'Oh, yes, sir,' Leah said, glancing across the room where Josiah was looking at her. She nodded her head briefly in his direction. As she carried the heavy tray out of the room, she heard Mr Fife Angas say to Thomas McGilvrey, 'What was that about oysters, Thomas?'

'Remind me to tell you about it another time,' McGilvrey replied. 'By Jove, I do believe the carpenter fellows are bringing the coffin up the stairs right now.'

Chapter 17

'What's wrong?' Leah asked, keeping her voice low and glancing back at the Lawson house where lights showed in every room. She caught a rank scent from the sea mixed with the smell of Josiah's Cuban cigar. He was pulling on the lower branches of a young coconut tree which rustled softly.

'Come here, Leah,' he said, pulling her against his chest. 'I won't be able to keep my promise,' he whispered in her ear. 'I feel terribly guilty.'

Leah drew back and saw in his eyes a mixture of regret and relief. Had relief been the first expression in his eyes? Was that why she herself felt shame, anger and sorrow?

'What do you mean?' Leah asked, rubbing her arms. She'd begun to feel cold. She looked up at the stars, reminding herself that it was the hurricane season and a starry sky was no indication of continued good weather in September.

'I'll be going away soon, to England or Scotland or some-where to study; whatever can be arranged.'

'To study what, Josiah?' Leah thought of the large oval mahogany table in his home, of the candles in gleaming glass shades. She thought of him reading, seated in a low chair, his feet stretched out on a red, grey and black rug with intricate geometric patterns.

'I don't know. I don't even want to go. My father has suggested medicine in Scotland or maybe law in England. I haven't had a chance to think about what I want to do.'

'When did all this come about?'

'During the crisis with the Spanish. He doesn't think we've seen the last of these skirmishes. He wants us to go away for a while.'

'Did you...' she hesitated. 'Did you ask him...?'

'I did. I asked him to assist me with the cost of your

emancipation and to help me to marry you.'

'What did he say?' Leah asked, thinking of his father's large red face, his small eyes, his sly, suggestive smile and his lips wet as if he'd only just run the tip of his tongue over them. He swaggered around the town in a wide-brimmed straw hat like an old-time buccaneer.

'Father? He didn't say much, just squinted at me in that way he has. Then he said, "Don't expect me to countenance and finance that scheme of yours."'

'You needn't go away, Jos. Couldn't you do something on your own? Maybe start in a small way, I mean.'

'Doing what, Leah?' He seemed surprised at the thought.

'Maybe you could try to get a mahogany works. Your father would respect that... maybe in time...'

'He doesn't want me in his line of business. Father's been spreading around his disapproval to high and low. My mother has talked to her friends, the chaplain and the superintendent.'

'What did they say?' Leah sat down on the ground and leaned her head against Josiah's knees. She felt so exhausted from the long day and the night that seemed unending. There would be no rest until the funeral was over tomorrow morning.

'I don't know what the chaplain said, probably the usual pious things. However, I did go and speak with the superintendent himself, who is a Christian man. I thought he would be sympathetic, persuade my parents to my view and all that. Instead he wrote me a strong letter and had his clerk copy it to my parents. My father says I am making my mother ill with anxiety and if I continue on my present course, he'll leave me out of his will.'

'Would he really do that, Jos?' Leah asked, thinking of his mother, Dorinda Potts, who it was said had African ancestry. However, she was very light skinned and had inherited several mahogany works upriver.

'I'm sure he would. He says I must think what my marriage

to you would mean to the future prospects of the family.'

'Ah,' Leah said, thinking that this then was the end. She understood Josiah much better now than she had in the early days when he'd lent her books and talked about making their way through the world together.

Leah knew that Josiah would not be able to abandon his freedom to travel about the settlement on his horse, order books, musical instruments and all the other things he considered essential from the merchants in town or overseas.

'We could go together to see the chaplain, try again, I mean.' Leah knew his answer before he replied.

'The chaplain is not in any position to go against the superintendent, Leah. Reverend Burke is dependent on the superintendent for his living.'

'Did you bring the superintendent's letter with you? I'd like to read it.'

She allowed Josiah to draw her close and for a moment she rested her head on his shoulder, wishing it was like the first time it had happened, when everything was still before them.

He took a deep breath and said, 'I'll just read the paragraph that concerns us and you'll see Leah that I did try. I can't let this letter leave my possession.'

'We can see by the light in the Angas' windows. Let's cross the road,' Leah said.

'I don't want you to be hurt,' Josiah said, 'but here goes. In the last paragraph, the superintendent wrote, "*Josiah, the connection you formed is neither honourable nor creditable and I suppose it would not require so great an effort as crossing the Atlantic to emancipate yourself from the fascinating charms of a female negro slave. The settlement unhappily has long laboured under great moral darkness and the connections such as you have formed, I am aware, have not been infrequent, nor held so dishonourable as they should have been, but I trust, through the mercy of God, that the light of the Gospel is beginning to dawn amongst us and its influence will no longer allow such degrading vice to endure amongst those who profess Christianity.'"*

There was a silence between them as they listened to the swish-swishing of the waves on the shore and to the branches of the coconut trees moving back and forth above their heads.

'It was you then, Josiah, who suggested that you had to leave to get away from me?'

'I told my parents that, yes, hoping they would not want me to leave.'

'But they took you at your word and so did the superintendent.'

'Yes.' He placed his arms around her shoulders and pulled her head against his chest. Her white headscarf fell off and she watched the breeze blow it through the darkness to the shore, where the waves dragged it to and fro, its ends floating out like little fishes.

Josiah had betrayed everything she felt he had encouraged her to believe in. Had she, in her own mind, in her own need, built up a Josiah who did not really exist? To Leah, the thought was devastating. She rescued her scarf from the surf and squeezed it dry. Frightened of his power to hurt her even more, she avoided his outstretched hand.

'I'd better get back, Josiah,' she said. 'I promised to help clean up in the kitchen and I need to help my mother with her bath. She hasn't been well all day.'

'I brought you a little present, Leah,' he said, holding out a box to her, 'to remember me by.' His voice was low and regretful but there was a finality to it that was unmistakable.

When Leah hesitated, he placed it into her apron pocket.

'I'll return your book,' Leah said.

'The book was a gift, Leah. Please keep it.'

'When are you leaving?'

'On one of the merchant ships loading up now... in a few

days, at most, but I'll try to see you before then.'

Leah didn't reply. She kissed him on the cheek and started running back to her duties at the wake for Marshall Lawson. At that moment, it didn't seem to her like it was really the end – that she wouldn't see Josiah again. However, as the night wore on and the dishes piled up and the din in the yard grew louder and louder, she felt bereft, as though she was sailing in a boat at night without a pilot to guide her through the treacherous channels of the barrier reef.

Chapter 18

After a while, Leah slipped out of the kitchen and tried to walk without undue haste across the bridge and down the stairs, where it seemed to her the pounding of drums had increased in intensity. Sukie and a number of other women were still serving drinks and food to late arrivals. Her mother was standing by the enormous fire-hearth, poking sticks of wood beneath the water pans Leah had put on to heat up for her mother's bath.

'Did you pay your respects?' Hannah asked, her face drawn, her lips pressed into a thin line. She didn't look up from the fire burning in the hearth.

'No, Mama. I haven't had time but I will do it before the coffin is closed.'

'I was looking for you a while ago. Did you leave the yard?'

'Yes,' Leah said, the heat from the fire making her break out in a sweat. 'Mama Hannah,' she said. 'Oh Mama. Josiah, Mama, Josiah.'

'I expected something like this,' Hannah said. 'I saw you talking with him. I made excuses to cook for you.'

Hannah drew Leah to the rear of the huts and held her close. She caressed her hair and said, 'I know all about it, my pet, all about it.'

They sat down on the ground with their backs against the hut, while Leah, one hand over her mouth, sobbed against her mother's shoulder.

After a while Leah sat up and, remembering Josiah's gift, she removed it from her pocket and gave it to her mother, who opened the box. Leah stared down at a delicate golden bracelet composed of tiny solid hearts alternating with the empty outlines of hearts. Her chest heaved and she sobbed quietly, unable to believe her eyes.

'Hmm,' her mother said, balancing the chain on a forefinger.

'He's being honest, though I doubt he had the sense to realize it. I am sure this wasn't meant to hurt you in any way, Leah. Hold up child. He needed to buy a gift and this bracelet was to hand, that's all.'

Leah watched the bracelet glinting in the light from the fire-hearth. 'It feels as though he was paying me off.'

'Maybe this was his way of trying to help you in some way, to buy your freedom, I mean. You've been saving up for that day.'

'But he said he wanted us to get married one day.'

'Ah, well. He probably meant it at the time. I think you should put this in your bundle. One day it might come in handy if you get a chance to buy your manumission. That would please me more than anything, Leah. To have a daughter who is free. That would be a blessing to us all.'

'I know, Mama. I know,' Leah said. 'But I never want to see it again.'

Hannah placed the bracelet on the purple velvet lining of the box. 'I'll hold it for you. You might feel differently after a while.'

'Let's lift the pans off the fire,' Leah said, getting to her feet. 'The water is ready now.'

She helped her mother to carry the pans to the wash-house and while Hannah was bathing, Leah walked out of the compound, down the lane to the sea shore.

She stayed there for a long while, looking up and down the Foreshore, hoping to see Josiah, hoping that he had changed his mind. She slipped off her boots and walked into the waves, which lapped soothingly around her ankles. To her left, the pier stretched into the sea. She was sweating and felt that a swim near the shore would help her feel better. She struck out, swimming swiftly through the gently rolling waves. Tired, she turned on her back and began floating, looking up at the sky, where the stars were beginning to fade. It would soon be morning, she thought to herself. When the sun rose, she would swim back to the shore. She felt drowsy and closed her eyes for a while, thinking of Josiah in the merchant ship sailing away to a new life.

It seemed as though she had closed her eyes for only a moment, when she felt someone thrashing in the waves beside her. Someone grabbed her shoulders and began pulling her through the waves. She couldn't make out who it was until they reached the shallows. It was Thomas McGilvrey and he was swearing terrible oaths at her. On the shore she saw her mother and Sam who was shouting, 'You got her, Master McGilvrey.'

Hannah waded through the water and helped her onto the shore. She laid her down on the sand as Leah vomited sea water. 'Oh, Mama,' Leah said, 'he said he loved me. He promised.'

She heard a sound like a laugh and saw Thomas McGilvrey looking down at Hannah and herself.

'You know what people say,' McGilvrey said to Leah. 'I saved your life, so now I own you.'

'I want to be free,' Leah said.

'Ay,' McGilvrey said, 'there's the rub.'

He walked off towards the Lawson compound, removing his wet clothing as he went.

'You should have thanked him,' Hannah said.

'I was only swimming for a while,' Leah said.

Chapter 19

Leah lay wide-eyed on her pallet in her family's room in the slave quarters at Overpond. The night-time sounds seemed magnified, the tap-tap of a cobbler's hammer, the wail of the baby in the next room and the breathing of her mother and brother on the floor beside her. Since that night a week ago, when Thomas McGilvrey had prevented her from drowning, Hannah and Sam had become a little distant, wary, watchful.

It was difficult to accept that partly because of her actions, her mother was growing increasingly timid, her eyes filled with unspoken anguish. Sam sometimes met her eyes but only reluctantly, as though he was scared of what he might see. Her mother was bearing up under a double burden; it was hard not to think of Sam's imminent future, working in the bush, wearing little or no clothing, for all intents and purposes lost to them for ten or eleven months each year.

She thought of confiding in Will but the old days, like the ones upriver, were gone. To Leah they seemed to be travelling on different paths, each by-way muddy and filled with sharp stones. By now he would know that his master, Thomas McGilvrey, had saved her from drowning herself, although that had not been her deliberate intention. She dared not imagine what Will would think about her actions.

Leah was grateful to Thomas McGilvrey but his rescue left her feeling vulnerable and in great debt to him. She was embarrassed to even think of what she had said to Hannah about Josiah as she lay gasping for air on the shore. She felt puzzled and confused by the change in her feelings towards Thomas McGilvrey. Why had he risked his own life to save hers? Why hadn't he sent Will or any of the slaves at the wake that night? She resolved to thank him at some future time.

'I don't want to continue feeling trapped like this,' she said to herself, 'fearing everyone I know, who must think I have lost my bearings. Why else would I have been floating so far out to sea?' It had not seemed to her that she had been in danger or at any great distance from the shore.

She had to accept that if she had unconsciously put herself in danger, then there were parts of her character that she had not known existed. It was odd to feel that she must now be on constant guard against herself. A slight breeze blew through the open window and she felt the sweat drying on her forehead, face and arms.

The better part of herself, Leah felt, was now becoming brittle and full of frightening echoes, like the noises she'd heard in the shimmering crystal caves Will had once shown her. She shifted to her side, gazing at the bit of sky she could see through the window, trying to still the anxiety that was beginning to radiate through her body from the base of her spine.

Earlier that night she and Hannah had been preparing a meal of yams and fish in the yard to the rear of the room in which they lived. Leah had turned from pounding the yams with a mortar and pestle to see Hannah leaning against the washing bowl, her soiled apron covering her face, weeping silently as though her heart was breaking.

Leah had held her close, trying to reassure her, 'I'm all right, Mama. We'll be all right.' Hannah's tears seemed unstoppable. Over her mother's heaving shoulders, Leah gazed at the bright moon above the coconut and golden plum trees growing on the edges of the swamp.

Hannah wiped her face with the tail of her apron and said, 'Time and again I've told you not to look at the moon when it's full, but you never listen, your ears are hard.'

'I'm sorry, Mama,' Leah said. 'Do you think that I was trying to drown myself?'

'I don't know what to think, Leah. Master McGilvrey, Miss

Sheba and some of the others feel that maybe you were.'

'I wasn't trying to drown myself, Mama.'

'I don't want to think anything like that, Leah.'

'Mama, I need you and Sam to believe me.'

As they ate that night from a shared bowl, Leah wondered why she could not love Will instead of Josiah who, without uttering a word or noticing her in any way, had captured her heart and imagination from the first moment she saw him entering the gate at his parents' home.

That night she began to list the people who had seriously affected her life. On one side she placed what she called the good people like her mother, Sam, Will, the Clare sisters and the Angas brothers. On the other she placed Graham Lawson, Josiah and his family and people like Eboe George, the fish vendor at the market, who always served her last. She didn't know where to put Thomas McGilvrey, who was a slaveowner, so she started a separate in-between category with him at the top of the list.

Before now her nights had usually been filled with dreams of gaining her freedom and her marriage to Josiah during some future December, when the weather was cool and almost everyone was in a mood for celebration. It was the time of year when the slaves and mahogany merchants would return from the bush to Belize Town for the Christmas season. Every year, during these weeks, many of the merchants drank and gambled away their earnings and mahogany concessions.

Now there would be no freedom and no quiet wedding in the presence of a magistrate friend of Josiah's father.

These realities were difficult to think about and to accept. She railed against them in her heart. 'It's not fair, it's cruel,' she thought to herself. 'Why was I born a slave?'

Except for the brief time she'd shared with Josiah, when had her life ever been free of everything she was now railing against? When had she not borne these harsh realities with as much courage as she could muster, endured them with a philosophical tilt to her chin and a combative gleam in her eyes? She'd usually said to employers, 'Yes, mam' and 'no, sir,' with exquisite courtesy. With Josiah's promises in her heart, it had been easier to say, 'One day, I won't need to say or do this any more. I'll be a free woman, with a home, children and my own industry.'

The memory of these familiar words made her smile briefly in the dark as she listened to the wind rustling the trees in the swamp and the continuous tap-tap-tapping of the cobbler's hammer. The baby next door was still crying.

Over the years the words had echoed automatically, like the memory of a tune which drifts through the mind. But now the words lining up side by side, like soldiers in a firing squad, no longer had the power to soothe the pain which suffused her mind. 'I'm a fool,' she said to herself, 'everybody else could see what I didn't.' Why had she thought she could escape the fate of her mother and her grandmother and so many other women she knew simply by willing it to happen?

She had tried to prepare herself for a future different from theirs. She had not displayed her hair in public but kept it wrapped up in her scarf made from squares of flour sacking. She did not wear off-the-shoulder dresses nor lift her skirts in the streets, no matter how muddy and filthy they were, to show off a red petticoat and a well-turned ankle.

She still felt like a modest woman who had hoped that hard work, a little reading, a little writing and her domestic skills would somehow release her from bondage.

Josiah had said that they would go away, maybe to Half-Moon Caye where they could live without the censure and contempt of the settlers. He had taught her one important lesson; his weaknesses would never permit him to marry simply because he loved someone. Josiah, most probably, would never marry for love alone.

If their situations had been reversed, would she have given up everything for someone her family did not want in their lives? Leah did not yet know the answer to her question and so it made Josiah's actions a little easier to bear. In time, perhaps she would be able to forget her own folly.

Leah moved from side to side on the frayed quilt rumpled beneath her body. There was little hope of sleep. She tiptoed to a corner of the room, turned up the wick of the lamp and opened her bundle of possessions. Unrolling the white, rectangular silk scarf – a gift from Josiah – she looked at the flyleaf of the book he had insisted she keep. Under the name *Robinson Crusoe* by Daniel Defoe it said, 'To Leah from Josiah.' She held the book, bound in red leather, against her face before turning again to page one. Her lips moved as she silently spelled out the words, '*I was born in the year 1632, in the City of York, of a good family, tho' not of that country, my father being a Foreigner of Bremen, who settled first at Hull.*'

By the time Leah had reached the bottom of the first page, she began to feel drowsy. Turning down the wick of the lamp, she crept back to her pallet. Feeling strangely comforted, she cradled the book in her arms and fell asleep.

Chapter 20

1800

It was a Saturday afternoon in January and Leah was folding laundry at the home of the Clare sisters. She had spent the chilly morning hours outdoors, washing and drying clothing and bed linen. Their lives hadn't changed very much during the last few months, except that she, Hannah and Sam were now owned by Thomas McGilvrey, whose claims to Graham Lawson's property had been authorized by the magistrates. The Clare sisters talked of little else. Leah wondered at times if they had expected to receive a legacy from Graham Lawson.

'The poor man died thinking he was being poisoned,' Miss Roslyn said, bending her head over the ruching on the bodice of a baby's christening gown. The afternoon sunshine from the nearby window brightened the strands of grey in her black hair. 'Of course, he must have been hallucinating. All that drink would kill anybody.'

The Clare sisters had visited Graham Lawson regularly. They'd purchased hog's lard ointment from the apothecary's shop to ease the pain of his bed sores and spent hours at his bedside talking with him and urging him to pray for his immortal soul.

'He told me,' Miss Evelyn said, 'that he was certain some form of wickedness was being practised on him.' She held the creamy white satin christening cap on one fist, twirling it this way and that, examining it closely in the light streaming through the jalousie blinds.

'You won't believe this, Leah,' Miss Roslyn said, 'but he wanted me to find slaves who could perform ceremonies to cure him. As if I knew anything about herb baths and sacrificing fowl and what not.'

To Leah it was a familiar story in the settlement – illness and misfortunes were often blamed on the practice of obeah, in which many people believed. As far as she could make out these secret rituals required grave-dirt, fresh animal blood, feathers, hair, dolls, herbs, oils, corked bottles, charms and incantations.

'The sound of the drums at night really bothered him,' Miss Roslyn said. 'He thought obeah men and women were surrounding his house. He became very superstitious at the end. Poor soul.'

Both women seemed lost in thought and it was silent in the bedroom for a while. Miss Roslyn rose from her chair and spread the satin christening gown on the bed, which was covered now with an embroidered white quilt. Turning back the hem of the gown, she examined her minute stitches.

Leah listened to the rattle of the seashell chimes on the verandah overlooking Haulover Creek and every now and then she heard the squeaking of the swing held up by chains anchored in the ceiling. Leah closed the cupboard doors and went to sit on a stool near the four-poster bed. She put her hands in the pocket of her apron and held tightly to the little bundle she'd kept there all day, hoping she'd be able to gather up the courage to speak.

Miss Evelyn looked at her over her spectacles and asked, 'Feeling all right, Leah? You look as if you are about to faint.' She took the bottle of smelling salts from the small table at her elbow and passed it to Leah.

'I haven't fainted for a while now,' Leah said, sniffing the salts. During the past few months she'd suffered from headaches, a lack of appetite and a general disinterest in most things. Assisting with the laundry and cooking at the Angas brothers, was about as much as she could do during the working week.

'Thanks be to the Almighty,' Miss Evelyn said. 'Take care of your health, Leah.'

'I try as best I can, Miss Evelyn,' Leah said, thinking of the senna, the sorosi vine and the herbal mixtures made by Hannah that she'd had to drink during the past few months. Leah knew that something was wrong with her for she was nearly always sleepy and tired.

To turn up at the Clare sisters' every Saturday morning sometimes seemed more than she could bear, especially as they never mentioned Josiah's name nor the merry times they'd all spent together listening to him read from his new novels. The only reading the Clare sisters did nowadays was from their huge Bible, parts of which Leah found consoling, especially the stories about the women, many of whom seemed to have had a much worse time of it than she did.

Leah felt that the smelling salts had done her some good. Feeling a little restored, she returned the bottle and said, 'Excuse me, Miss Evelyn. I hope you won't be upset but I was wondering whether you and Miss Roslyn could... would buy something from me.'

'Buy something from you?' Miss Evelyn asked, removing her wire-rimmed glasses and peering at Leah.

'You heard what she said, Evelyn. Why must you parrot everything people say?'

'Parrot? Parrot?' Miss Evelyn heaved herself out of the chair. She placed the christening cap carefully down on the bed as though it was made of glass. 'Well now I've heard everything, Roslyn. As a Christian woman, I wouldn't lower myself to reply.'

'I didn't mean to say that, Evelyn. It just flew out of my mouth.'

'Never mind,' Miss Evelyn said, 'I'll go and make the tea. I wouldn't want Leah to faint from hunger.'

Miss Evelyn's footsteps echoed on the polished pinewood floor and they heard the bang of the dining-room door.

With a sigh, Miss Roslyn said, 'It was my turn to make the tea. I won't hear the end of that tonight.'

'I'm sorry,' Leah said, feeling as though she was diving through the murky waters of Haulover Creek.

'Oh, it's not your fault,' Miss Roslyn said. 'I think we are still in mourning for Marshall and Graham. We were distant relatives, you know.'

'I didn't know,' Leah said. She coughed to clear her throat.

'Oh well, few people do. Graham's father, Bertram, was out here before Graham was. Bertram was a very wealthy logwooder but that was a long time ago, in our parents' day.'

'What happened to Bertram Lawson?' Leah asked, looking at the beautiful mahogany four-poster bed.

'Well, first one thing and then another but in the end he sailed back to Scotland. Please don't tell Evelyn I told you.' Miss Roslyn placed her hand on Leah's arm and kissed her cheek.

'You know you can trust me,' Leah said. She loved the two sisters very much and understood better now why they continued to take such an interest in her affairs. Leah rubbed her eyes, trying not to cry.

'I don't want you to be sad about all that, Leah,' Miss Roslyn said. 'But you are a grown woman now. That is the story of most Creole people here.' She glanced down at Leah's tightly balled fist. 'What do you have in your hand?'

Leah opened the bit of cotton cloth and lifted from it the bracelet with its heavy clasp. It glittered in the sunlight. Feeling ashamed, she stared down at the linked hearts, listening to the intake of Miss Roslyn's breath. She seemed speechless.

'Tea,' Miss Evelyn called from the dining room. Her voice made them both jump.

Clutching the bracelet in her hand, Leah followed Miss Roslyn into the dining room where the table was laid for tea.

'Sit down, Leah,' Miss Roslyn said, pointing to the chair nearest the kitchen door.

Leah sat on the edge of her chair watching the steam rise from the cup which Miss Evelyn was filling with tea. The smell of the freshly baked bread made her feel slightly nauseous. She looked across the table at the empty chair in which Josiah had sat reading to them on those Saturdays long ago. She'd stopped hoping to get word of him through the Clare sisters but, as far as she knew, he hadn't written to them.

'Show Evelyn that bracelet,' Miss Roslyn said, pushing aside her plate of sliced bread spread thickly with guava cheese.

'What bracelet?' Miss Evelyn asked, spilling tea into her saucer.

'There you go again,' Miss Roslyn said, 'I said bracelet, a gold bracelet.'

'There's no need to raise your voice at me, Roslyn. Your nerves are going. You'd better drink some tonic later.' Miss Evelyn scraped back her chair and said to Leah, 'Do you want to sell a gold bracelet, Leah?' It seemed more than she could comprehend.

Leah placed it on the table where it looked out of place lying next to the fat brown teapot and an earthenware jug filled with stalks of croton. Their leaves, streaked with green and yellow, reminded Leah of how carefully she had selected them when Josiah was to visit. Everything seemed so familiar and yet so strange.

'Was this a parting bon?' Miss Evelyn asked. Her voice softened as she saw Leah wiping her face.

'We don't need to ask from whom, Evelyn, so just don't.' Turning to Leah, Miss Roslyn said, 'It's a lovely bracelet, my dear. Are you sure you want to sell it?'

Leah nodded. 'I never wanted it,' she said.

Miss Evelyn sighed. 'I wish we could afford to buy it Leah but it looks very expensive. I can't imagine where he got the money to pay for it.'

'Indeed,' Miss Roslyn said, shifting her eyes away from the bracelet.

Leah removed the bracelet and wrapped it up again in the cloth, knotting the ends tightly.

'What are you going to do with the money, if you do manage

to sell it?' Miss Roslyn asked.

'Well, Mama and I have some doubloons saved from extra work here and there. We thought we could buy freedom for Sam and myself.'

'Then what?' Miss Evelyn said.

'I thought maybe we could hire ourselves out to you, maybe to Mr Fife Angas and other people about the town.'

The women looked at her for a while, then at each other.

At last, Miss Roslyn said, 'Thomas McGilvrey might someday allow you to buy your freedom. I don't know about now, though. We saw him at the Angas brothers' last Sunday. Mr Fife Angas was talking about the brotherhood of man and the abolition of slave trading. He said it was the new spirit abroad in England.'

'I didn't hear Thomas McGilvrey agreeing, Roslyn. He said it would mean ruin for logwood and mahogany merchants like himself.'

'Still,' Miss Roslyn said, 'he didn't look completely opposed to the idea. He was just presenting the other side.'

'Have it your way, Roslyn,' Miss Evelyn said, beginning to pile up the cups and saucers. 'You can read people's minds as well as their faces nowadays.'

'I'm not looking for an argument, Evelyn,' Miss Roslyn said. 'We could try to sell the bracelet for Leah. We know a lot of people with money to buy that kind of thing, especially if we said it was for a good cause.'

'And what good cause were you thinking of, exactly?' Miss Evelyn asked.

'We could say it was for assisting new converts and Leah will soon want to be baptized, won't you, Leah?'

Leah swallowed and did not reply for a minute.

She thought of Sunday mornings and the settlers seated for the service in the Court House, while the slaves stood in the rear. She lifted her head and said with resolution, 'Yes, I do want to be baptized someday, Miss Roslyn.'

Miss Roslyn put out her hand and Leah placed in her palm her little bundle. It contained all her hopes and dreams for the future.

'It's getting late,' Miss Evelyn said. 'Shall we say Psalm 23?'

They bowed their heads and Miss Roslyn began, 'The Lord Is My Shepherd'.

Miss Evelyn and Leah replied, 'I shall not want.'

Chapter 21

Leah waited in suspense for the Clare sisters to tell her that, at last, they had sold the bracelet. However, Saturday after Saturday passed but still the sisters did not refer to the bracelet. The dry season came and went. So did the rainy season when everyone kept an eye out for hurricanes. No bad storms came that year and as December with its cooler weather approached, people turned with relief to their preparations for the Christmas season.

During the day and night, the streets filled up with free citizens, slaves, logwooders, mahogany cutters, merchants and the Waika Indians from the Miskito Shore.

On her way to the Clares' one Saturday in early December she saw, in the crowded market near Haulover Creek, a group of new immigrants who people said had never been slaves. It was an amazing sight to Leah and she slowed her pace to more closely observe the women in colourful head-ties and long skirts selling food they'd grown. She glimpsed plantains, bananas, large, flat disks of white cassava bread and starch made from cassava roots and she listened as the women spoke to each other in their own tongue. Leah marvelled at the strange language she'd heard as she paid for her passage in a dorey which would take her across the creek to the north side of the town.

When she entered the Clares' small house it was filled with the smell of black fruit cakes soaking in rum to keep them moist. Leah expected a busy day. The Clares liked to have the house cleaned early during the Christmas season. Old trunks and patakee baskets used for storage were pulled out, unpacked and repacked. She found the Clare sisters in the back yard re-varnishing their small tables and chairs. When they saw her, the sisters greeted her with smiles and bright eyes.

'Well, Leah,' Miss Evelyn said, 'we've sold the bracelet at last!' She untied a pouch from her waist, weighing it in her hand.

Miss Roslyn took the heavy leather pouch from her sister and placed it in Leah's hand. 'We got a good price for it. I hope you are pleased.'

'Oh, yes, thank you very much. I thought that maybe you couldn't sell it after all.' She hugged first Miss Evelyn and then Miss Roslyn, who both kept refusing to admit that they needed any thanks at all.

'No need for tears, Leah. With luck, you'll get your emancipation and Sam's. Other people we know are getting the gift of freedom this Christmas.'

'Who bought the bracelet?' Leah asked, tying the pouch around her waist and covering it with her long, baggy blouse.

'We can't tell you,' Miss Roslyn said, her smile fading a little.

'It was bought as a Christmas present for someone's wife,' Miss Evelyn said. 'We promised to keep it to ourselves.'

'Thank you again,' Leah said. 'I can't think when I've felt so relieved. It's a good day, the best I can remember.'

'Well, we know it,' Miss Roslyn said, 'and we have a Christmas present for you from us.'

'You are to go today to see Thomas McGilvrey. After lunch is a good time,' Miss Evelyn said. 'Rumour has it that he's had a good year with logwood and mahogany. Thousands of British pounds... it's all over town.'

'So he may be in a mood to be generous this Christmas season. We are praying for a miracle, anyway,' Miss Roslyn said.

'Do you think so?' Leah asked, feeling the blood growing hot in her cheeks. 'I couldn't go today,' she said, looking back to the house where everything inside was topsy-turvy.

'The house can wait,' Miss Roslyn said. 'The day is our gift to you.'

'Come inside,' Miss Evelyn said. 'We have something for you to put on.'

In the bedroom, spread out on the four-poster bed, was a

brown cotton dress and a large brown shawl with black fringes. 'Now,' Miss Evelyn said, 'change into this dress.'

Leah did as she was told and felt the dress slide easily over her body. It was loose around the waist as she had lost a lot of weight.

'That's what the shawl is for,' Miss Roslyn said. 'Tie it around your waist and let the knot rest on your hip. There, now don't you look fine.' She pushed Leah in front of the mirror hung above the chest of drawers.

Leah stared at her reflection, astonished at how different she looked. 'I can't go there looking like this,' she said.

'Yes, you can,' Miss Evelyn said. 'Don't put on your scarf. Just let your braid fall down your back. Like that, yes.'

'After all, you're not going as a beggar. You've got reals, pieces of eight and doubloons in that pouch, plus the money you and Hannah saved. Evelyn and I always try to look our best when we do business in town. Take your brogues off,' Miss Roslyn said, 'and put on these slippers. Your feet are smaller than mine but stuff these cotton balls into the toes.' She watched as Leah slipped her feet into the shoes.

Leah's knees felt as though they were about to buckle so she sat on the stool, feeling the smooth cotton dress falling softly around her knees and ankles. She ran a hand across her hair, grateful for the care with which Hannah braided it. There were no rough spots, no strands out of place. The string which tied the end of her plait was still in place but she re-tied it anyway, her fingers shaking.

The morning flew by quickly and she felt giddy with excitement, as though she already held her manumission paper signed, sealed and delivered. The sisters, in perfect amiability, had laughed, talked and prayed together as they'd tried to make her look as presentable as possible. But now they were staring at her, their arms folded, their eyes expectant. Their girlish glee, their daring, had subsided.

'You'd better make a start if you're going, Leah,' Miss Evelyn said looking at the small watch that hung on a chain around her neck.

They escorted Leah through the front door and onto the verandah where they sat on the wooden swing – moving it back and forth with their feet.

'Let us know as soon as you can, whatever happens,' Miss Roslyn said, looking down at her hands clasped tightly in her lap.

Leah nodded but did not reply. She felt their eyes on her back as she set off down the road. Overhead, wisps of cloud floated across a blue sky. She tried to distract herself by thinking of the new people she had seen at the market but, as usual, almost every street and lane reminded her of Josiah. Try as she might, she was unable to imagine what his life must be like in Scotland or England.

Her heart continued to beat too quickly and perspiration rolled down her face. The bodice of the brown dress was already soaked with sweat and dust covered the black cloth slippers which kept sliding off her feet.

The dreadful night when she'd been rescued by Thomas McGilvrey seemed like something that had happened to someone else. On holiday mornings, when the weather was right, she and Sam had continued to collect oysters from the creek. They carried them to the Lawson compound as an expression of gratitude to Thomas McGilvrey. On these occasions, they'd sometimes meet him walking on the road or riding his brown horse. One day in the garden, where he was setting out plant specimens on a rectangular unvarnished table, he'd said to them, 'Hello again. More oysters eh? I'm always glad to get them.' Turning to Leah, he asked, 'No more swimming at night, I hope?' He twisted the stem of a leaf in his hand as he observed her face closely.

'No sir,' Leah replied, wishing she could hear him sing again, like the first time they'd met him on the Foreshore.

'Glad to hear it,' Thomas McGilvrey said, patting her on the shoulder and turning back to his work.

So it had been, the odd word here and there, a smile between them, a friendliness to which Leah and Sam soon became accustomed.

When Graham Lawson had died, her mother had been in attendance and she and Sam had helped at the wake, serving food and drink and helping to clean up in the kitchen, much as they had done when his son, Marshall, had met his death at the Battle of St George's Caye.

Still, how was she to go there, to face Thomas McGilvrey and proffer money for her freedom and for Sam's? She wondered whether she'd have the courage to go through with it. She thought of Hannah and Sam, wondering what would happen if Thomas McGilvrey refused to free them, if she did manage to speak with him. It was a fairly long walk but it seemed to her that all too quickly she had reached the Foreshore.

Leah walked down the lane to the house with the green shutters. The shop on the ground floor was now open and the British clerk, a dark-haired young man, was displaying a pair of drill trousers to a settler, short and bow-legged, jingling keys on a chain in his hand. In this store Graham Lawson had once sold quantities of ale, port and wine, brandy and rum, coffee, sugar, raisins and imported foodstuffs like olives, capers and salad oil.

There had been, so Leah had heard, displays of various types of vests, fine cotton shirts, neckerchiefs, handkerchiefs and silk hose. For a long time before Graham Lawson's death it had been said everywhere in town that his stock was 'scanty' as he had no money to pay his overseas creditors.

Leah prayed that Will had not yet come downriver from Roaring Creek. How would she explain to him her borrowed costume and scarf, her bare head and the neat slippers on her feet? She tinkled the bell and Miss Sheba called from the kitchen, 'Who is it?' The impatience in her voice made it sound high and sharp.

'It's Leah, come to see Mr McGilvrey,' Leah said. Mealtimes were the worst time to visit as Thomas McGilvrey might have guests for lunch. She might have to wait, which would be all right as she needed time to think.

Miss Sheba pushed her head through the kitchen window and for a moment looked nonplussed. 'It's you, Leah,' she said. 'For a minute, I almost didn't recognize you in that frock. The gate isn't locked.'

As she entered the compound, Leah saw the brown and white dogs, Jip and Merry, penned up underneath the house, their dark eyes gleaming between the planks which were covered with wire meshing. They ran around and around the white shell sand on the ground, their tails fanning the air. Each bark seemed like a blow to her chest. She hurried around the corner of the house and up the stairs disturbing two cats, the colour of golden marmalade, sunning themselves on the wooden bridge to the outside kitchen.

Chapter 22

As she approached the kitchen door, Leah smelt conch fritters frying. She could hear them sizzling in the pan as Miss Sheba turned several over to brown in coconut oil. She put her head out of the kitchen door and said, 'If you're coming in, come in, Leah. I don't have all day, you know.'

'Thank you, mam,' Leah said, looking at the pile of grated coconut on the counter. After adding water, Miss Sheba would squeeze the coconut meat to produce milk which she used for baking bread and for cooking rice and beans.

'Does your poor ma know you are visiting here today?' Miss Sheba asked, shaking the pan over the fire-hearth.

'No, mam,' Leah said, watching as Miss Sheba lifted a fritter out of the pan. She allowed the oil to drip from the fritter before laying it on a plate. From a hook, Miss Sheba took a clean cloth and patted the fritter.

She frowned. 'You are a brave girl, no mistake about it, to come here on your own. Sit on that stool by the door and cool off.' She dipped a cup into a bucket of water on the counter and gave it to Leah.

'Thanks, mam,' Leah said, glancing through the doorway. The royal palms and coconut trees swayed in the breeze. She felt the sweat drying on her face and arms and wished she could stretch herself out on the grass beneath the trees and drift into sleep. It would be a forgetting kind of sleep there, far from the noise and stench of the rooms in which she and her family now lived.

'Are you hoping for something from Master McGilvrey?' Miss Sheba asked, her eyes speculative.

Leah nodded, her heart beating fast. She listened to the clip-clopping of a horse along the street. She wondered if the rider and horse were from next door where Josiah's family lived and where she had once worked as an assistant to the laundress.

She could almost see Josiah's slender brown hands gripping the reins, hands that were used mostly for reading and writing. She thought of his narrow face, the redness of his mouth against his skin, the shiny blackness of his moustache and neatly trimmed beard and his jet black eyebrows, bushy and arched over his expressive dark eyes with long lashes.

Leah stood up and walked to the back window, noting that the windows of the slave rooms were all shuttered. Each of the rooms was twice the size of the one in which she lived with her mother and Sam. Golden plum and tamarind trees shaded the thatched roofs.

'Are you hoping to shift rooms?' Miss Sheba asked, wrapping a clean apron around her body. 'It'd be a big help to have you, Hannah and Sam here.'

Leah did not reply. She drank some more water from the cup and returned to the stool by the door. Miss Sheba seemed not to have noticed her silence for she said, 'The accommodation is only your due and Master McGilvrey must know it, even if Master Lawson, God rest his soul, did not allow the truth.'

Leah drank more water and looked down at her feet encased in Miss Evelyn's black slippers.

'When I take in the lunch, I'll tell Master McGilvrey you're here to see him,' Miss Sheba said. 'I won't mention anything about the rooms. I'll leave that to you.' She handed Leah a fritter on a plate and some more water in the large tin cup.

'I don't mind waiting,' Leah said, her stomach heaving as she looked down at the fritter. When Miss Sheba had disappeared into the house with her laden tray, Leah threw the fritter into the yard. The waiting cats rushed down the stairs after it and Leah went back to sit on the stool by the door. Would Thomas McGilvrey agree to see her? At that moment, she wished that he would suggest that she return some other day.

Chapter 23

As Leah walked across the bridge, Miss Sheba's voice and the noises in the kitchen receded. She heard hammering and muted voices in the main house. Pushing against the heavy door, she entered the dining room. The rectangular rugs, with patterns in grey and black, were gone from the polished pinewood floorboards.

Beyond the mahogany archway three male slaves and two female slaves, including Berry, the cook's assistant, were wrapping Graham Lawson's personal effects with cloth and sacking. They would be packed into trunks and crates for shipment to Scotland or England. Leah had never quite been able to determine in which country Graham Lawson had been born.

She glanced at the open drawers of his desk and the empty spaces on the wall behind it. Graham Lawson's family pictures had been removed. The heavy silver candle sticks were missing, as well as the long rectangular picture of a man fishing in a rushing stream which had hung on the wall above the sideboard.

'You're to go out on the verandah, Leah,' Berry said, cradling a glass decanter in her hand. She smiled at Leah as though from now on they shared a secret. 'Master McGilvrey is waiting,' she said.

On the verandah Thomas McGilvrey was seated at a table with various thick account books at his elbow.

He was rubbing his cheek with the feather of a quill pen and reading the papers in front of him. His long brown hair was parted in the middle and he wore a dark jacket, a fawn-coloured waistcoat and tan breeches.

'Good afternoon, sir,' Leah said. It was a busy time of the afternoon and she listened to the braying of mules and the rattle of cart wheels.

'Yes?' He said, looking up. 'Oh, it's you. I could have sworn cook told me it was Hannah.'

'That's my mother's name,' Leah said, shifting from one foot to the other. She noticed the lines on his forehead, the grey in his bushy eyebrows and his hands, speckled with brown spots. The faint scent of his hair perfume mingled with the scent of ink and the salty air from the sea.

'And your brother's name is Sam. Will has been telling me about your family,' he said, using a square of black cloth to wipe the nib of his pen. He closed the inkpot and leaned back in his chair observing her closely.

'Is Will here, sir?' Leah asked, her heart thumping. She looked out to sea, almost dead calm, trying to subdue her nervousness and her desire to excuse herself and leave.

'Not as yet, but he'll be paddling in soon with the other lads. We've had a busy year,' he said, placing a glass paperweight on his papers and straightening his blotter.

'Please accept my thanks again, sir, for saving my life that night,' Leah said.

He smiled. 'I hope you think my effort was worth the trouble. It doesn't do, you know, to die for love.'

'No, sir, I understand some things better now.'

'So do I,' Thomas McGilvrey said. 'I remember the feeling very well. I once believed that everything was well lost for love and all that.'

He looked at her as though he expected some reaction so Leah asked, 'Do you remember that from when you were young, sir?' Looking at his bent head, Leah noticed that his hair at the temples was thinner than she remembered.

'I'm not that old,' Thomas McGilvrey said, rubbing his chin which had a cleft in it. 'But I've knocked about a bit and I've had my share of heartbreak. Everyone does, sooner or later.'

'I expect that must be true, sir,' Leah said. 'Do you have a family?' She thought it must be strange for him, living in a foreign country without his own people.

'I had a wife and a son,' McGilvrey said, his face growing red. 'But that was all a long time ago. I don't like to speak about it.'

'No, sir,' Leah said, looking out to sea, which was like grey silk, as the sun had gone behind the clouds. She drew in a deep breath and was about to speak but Thomas McGilvrey said, lowering his voice, 'I did want to talk with you, Leah, so I'm glad you're here.' He got up and walked across the verandah to the door and said, 'Berry, please bring some tea and biscuits, if cook has any.'

He lifted a chair and set it down in front of the table. Taking her elbow, he urged Leah to sit down.

Leah felt extremely uneasy sitting on the edge of her chair, watching Thomas McGilvrey's hands moving across the table, gathering up papers and memorandum books. She listened to his breathing and when she looked up he was watching her as he ran a finger up and down his long nose which jutted out from his face. His eyes were bloodshot and his face looked haggard, as though it had been a long time since he'd had a good night's sleep.

'Did you want to ask me something?' Leah asked, to break the silence.

'Yes. I am in the middle of taking inventory of Graham Lawson's possessions, paying his debts and packing up his personal effects to be shipped to his relatives in Scotland.'

'Yes, I can see,' Leah said. 'I was wondering, sir, if I could ask you something, if you don't mind, about Sam and myself.'

'About Graham Lawson's will, you mean?'

'Oh, no sir,' Leah said, growing alarmed. Did he think she had hoped to receive her freedom or a legacy from Graham Lawson?

'All his property belongs to me now but I intend to provide for you, Sam and Hannah. It's only right. I can see Graham Lawson's face each time I look at you.' He smiled.

Leah's spirits rose a little and she held the money pouches firmly in her hand. She looked down at her hands and tucked her feet underneath the straight-backed chair with curved legs which she recognized as one from the dining room.

'Well?' Thomas McGilvrey asked and when Leah did not reply he continued, 'The rooms in the house are fairly comfortable and cook needs some help. She's going a bit blind, although she won't admit it.'

Leah untied her two pouches of money from her waist and placed them in her lap, listening to Thomas McGilvrey as he talked about his plans for the future. His eyes had a kindly expression in them as he looked at Leah.

'I have great faith in Will,' Thomas McGilvrey said, 'and he tells me you and your family are the most reliable people I could find. Besides, I like the three of you very much.'

'We like you too, sir,' Leah said.

'Later on I may have the house re-decorated. You could have your own room in due course, and a nice wardrobe. You and Hannah will know better than I do how these things are arranged.'

'Excuse me, sir, but I hoped to talk with you about something else, sir, if you don't mind,' Leah said, holding the pouches tightly in her hands.

'Have I left anything out?' He smiled again, looking at her almost anxiously.

'No, sir,' Leah said, 'I am here to ask you to kindly grant me my manumission – and Sam's.'

She looked up at Thomas McGilvrey, who had stood up. As she looked into his eyes, she was again reminded of sunshine glinting on the green bottles in the apothecary's shop. Perhaps because of what he had intimated before, she was no longer nervous. She sat up straighter in her chair, holding the money that she knew was more than enough to purchase their freedom.

Thomas McGilvrey leaned against the verandah railing, his arms folded. A slight breeze blew his hair forward and Leah thought she caught a whiff of brandy on his breath as he bent towards her.

'But Leah, I want you to stay. I didn't risk my health pulling you out of the sea to have you leave. You must have guessed that I am very fond of you.'

'Thank you again, sir,' Leah said, putting the money on the table. 'I don't expect you to gift us our freedom. This money is enough to pay for Sam and me.'

'Well, it is Christmas time and you are Graham Lawson's daughter. If you want your freedom, you shall have it,' Thomas McGilvrey said. He paced up and down the verandah, his hands clasped behind his back.

'And Sam's?' Leah asked, her heart racing. She couldn't believe that it had been that easy.

'And Sam's,' Thomas McGilvrey said, 'on certain conditions, of course. I intend to have you and your family here, even if we have to make some other arrangement.'

Leah stood up, feeling alarmed. Had he been joking after all? She picked up the pouches and pulled the drawstrings tightly.

McGilvrey put his hands on her shoulder, looking into her eyes. His face was serious. 'If I give you your freedom, you will need to agree to marry me – a licence, magistrate and all that.'

'You don't have to do that, sir,' Leah said, feeling chilled to the bone. She understood now why her mother had always said that she shouldn't meet with the settlement owners or their wives by herself. She wished she hadn't been in such a fever of excitement and hope. If she'd waited another day, Sam would have been able to be here with her.

She looked around her, hoping to see Berry emerging from the house with the tea tray. Then she'd be able to make her excuses. This had been such a mistake. She understood very well what Thomas McGilvrey had said and she didn't believe it.

'Excuse me, sir, I'll be going now if you don't mind,' Leah said, thinking of the Clare sisters who were waiting to learn the outcome of her visit.

'If you don't stop calling me sir, I think I'll go mad,' Thomas McGilvrey said.

'Then I won't,' Leah replied, stifling the bitter words that she wanted to say. He had been so nice, had said he would free them and now he was mocking her, knowing that she'd wanted to marry Josiah.

McGilvrey took one of her hands and placed it in his. He held it gently and said, 'It's a bargain, like many made every day by people all over the world. You will take care of my property when I am away and be my companion when I am at home. In return, you'll have freedom, shelter and protection for you and your family.' He tilted her chin so that he could look into her eyes.

'I'd like to buy our freedom,' Leah said, looking up at him, trying to read his expression. 'I'd feel better and we'd be more than glad to work here.'

'But then you'd be free to come and go,' Thomas McGilvrey said. 'Who knows? You might get a better offer, someday.'

'We wouldn't leave,' Leah said, feeling as though she was fighting for her life with few weapons to hand, 'if you treated us well.'

'I'm not willing to take that chance on the future,' Thomas McGilvrey said. 'I'm not young any more and I want to marry, settle down and have a family.'

'Why don't you go home to find another wife?' Leah asked, wishing she could remove her hand from his without giving offence.

McGilvrey pressed her hand to his lips, which felt cool and smooth. 'If the truth must be told, I hope never to return.'

'Why not?' Leah asked, wondering whether he'd committed a crime. She'd heard that hungry people in England could be hung for stealing a loaf of bread. Or perhaps he'd be put in jail for gambling debts. She shivered.

'Let's just say that I want a fresh start and I am hoping you'll help me to be the person I know I can be.'

'Is that all?' Leah asked, trying to sort out her thoughts. She knew she'd never be able to love anyone the way she loved Josiah. But she didn't think Thomas McGilvrey was asking her to love him. If he was serious about marrying her, she would do it. It was her only chance to gain freedom for herself, Hannah and Sam.

'I could try to be your friend,' Leah said, 'if you mean it, about marrying me I mean.'

'I do mean it,' Thomas McGilvrey said. 'I want to marry someone who is not remotely like my late wife. Maryanne was very dear to me, as was the child. I'd like another son.'

'How did they die?' Leah asked.

'We were on our way to Jamaica where we were to live. I was going there to take up a position on one of the sugar estates. It seems like another life now. They both became ill with fever and in a few days they were dead. We buried them at sea.'

'I am so sorry,' Leah said, her lips trembling, wishing she could think of words to comfort Thomas McGilvrey, who now had his face in his hands.

Leah's fingers still tingled from the contact with Thomas McGilvrey, who was old enough to be her father. How different he seemed to be from Graham Lawson, a proud, arrogant man who had really not even liked Hannah, Sam and herself. It was also extremely odd to think that, if McGilvrey was serious, she, Hannah and Sam would be living in Graham Lawson's compound.

Leah stretched out a hand and stroked McGilvrey's hair. 'Don't cry, sir, I mean, don't cry, Mr McGilvrey.' Leah heard the rattling of crockery and walked quickly to open the door and take the tea tray from Berry.

'Thank you,' Thomas McGilvrey said, wiping his eyes with a handkerchief. 'I have never spoken about those dreadful days.'

Leah poured him a cup of tea and he sipped it gingerly.

'Thank you,' he said again. 'We're friends already, I think.'

'Yes, we are,' Leah said, feeling consoled. She said a silent prayer to herself, one the Clare sisters had taught her. Perhaps prayers did work she thought, at least for some people.

'Don't you want the money?' Leah asked. 'It would make me feel better.'

He shook his head. 'All this could have been yours if Graham Lawson had left it to you and Sam in his will.'

'He didn't really think of us as his family. We didn't really know him very well, not even my mother.'

'Well, I hope to make up for all that,' Thomas McGilvrey said. 'Will you think about what I've said?'

'I've thought about it,' Leah said. 'I'd like to be free, marry you and have children.'

She heard Thomas McGilvrey chuckle.

'Why are you laughing?' Leah asked. She sat up straighter in her chair.

'You make me laugh,' he replied, 'and that's a good start.' He stretched his hand across the table and grasped her fingers.

'You won't let me down?' Leah asked, thinking of Josiah who had sworn he loved her, who had promised to marry her after they'd purchased her freedom.

'I won't let you down,' Thomas McGilvrey said. 'Will you let me down, Leah, in any way whatsoever?'

'I promise never to let you down,' Leah said, meaning it with all her heart.

Chapter 24

1807

At mid-morning one Monday in August, Leah was on her way to visit Sukie and to make a few purchases at the apothecary's shop, across the corner from Burnaby's Tavern at the far end of the Foreshore. The tavern had been named for a Captain Burnaby, long departed from the settlement. In 1765 he had drawn up a set of regulations by which the settlers had governed themselves, more or less, for generations.

It had rained heavily earlier that day so Leah stepped carefully around the puddles, twisting her pale cream parasol to shade her face from the fierce heat of the sun. She was missing her brother, Sam, gone for months upriver where he spent his days chopping off branches from felled mahogany logs at a McGilvrey camp near Roaring Creek.

It was hard to think of him, almost a man now, striding half-naked through the forests, his dark eyes sad and his face sombre. Accidents, fights, beatings, murders and other unspeakable events occurred frequently in the bush. She understood that her brother now knew dangerous secrets, like the routes of runaway slaves and the names of those who had facilitated their escape.

Thomas McGilvrey had not freed Sam as he'd promised, although he often said, 'Soon, soon, try to be patient.'

Thomas had gone back on his word to her and this had caused a strain in their relationship. She no longer trusted him as she once had done and this greatly saddened her.

Leah knew that Sam had to learn the mahogany trade and that he worked, some of the time, alongside Will and Sharper who did the best they could on his behalf. Still, she missed the old days when they'd wandered around the town and paddled up and down the creek fishing or catching crabs and collecting oysters.

Today Leah longed for his company more than ever as she was dreading facing Sukie again. Several weeks before in May, she'd entered the apothecary's shop, paused for a moment in the doorway and watched Sukie, who was dusting and cleaning. Leah had taken a deep breath, inhaling the scent of medicinal plants and tree barks mingling with the spicy scents of ginger, pepper, cloves and orange.

She'd watched as Sukie ran the feather duster over the wide mahogany counters, the porcelain jars and the wall cupboards with dozens of tiny brass-handled drawers, their contents labelled in a clear script. She was humming under her breath as she stood on tiptoe stretching her arm so that the duster could reach the wooden drawers above her head.

Leah hesitated to make her presence known, for just the sight of her seemed to irritate Sukie on the few occasions when they met. Leah closed the screen door, letting it slam behind her, and Sukie turned around, startled and annoyed.

'We don't open until eight,' she said, rearranging packets of toothbrushes, bottles of tinctures, oils, drops, bitters and an array of other bottles which Leah did not recognize.

'Good morning, Sukie,' Leah had said. 'I came early to see how you are doing.' She looked down at the paper in her hand. Listed there were packages of comfits, prunes and tobacco.

'What's good about it?' Sukie asked. 'You scared me.'

She rattled bedpans and urinals as she moved them along the shelves, dusting as she went. 'Spying on me now are you, Mistress McGilvrey?'

'Don't call me that,' Leah said, feeling her face growing hot with anger. She fanned her face with the sheet of paper in her hand.

'Why not? You're not really married then? Don't think that you are better than me just because you have a ring on your finger and live in Graham Lawson's house. He must be turning in his grave.'

138

'How can I think I am better than you, Sukie? You are a Miskito Indian and wrongly enslaved, aren't you? How could I forget?'

'I was in here minding my own business and now you come sneaking in here turning me into a pappyshow, laughing at me, eh?'

'Do you see me laughing?' Leah asked.

'I may only be an ignorant Indian wrongfully enslaved but I know very well that there's laugh and then there's laugh, the inside kind.'

'Ah, Sukie,' Leah said, 'I came by to see you because I heard a rumour that things weren't going well.' She tilted her head to indicate the floor above where Mistress Orissa Caslow and apothecary Preston Dickey lived.

Sukie paused, then picked up her broom. Its desultory scraping across the wooden floor, heavy footsteps overhead and the voices of men working outside filled the silence.

'Don't think you can butter up to me like you used to do, Leah. I'll tell Will you insulted me as soon as I see him.'

'Why Will?' Leah asked, surprised to feel her heart lurch. The last time she'd seen Will there'd been a change in him. He had become increasingly distant over the years. He looked a lot different too. His hair was receding slightly at the temples, exposing more fully his high, broad forehead. Will's wide smile was more confident but Leah thought that his eyes seemed to mock her. He walked around with a large, wrinkled handkerchief carelessly draped around his neck which made him seem almost reckless.

Early one morning, Leah had watched him at the water barrels, sluicing himself down, but she'd been too shy to call out easily to him as she used to do; she only had access now to Will the slave, the ace mahogany hunter, always willing to help out whenever he was around. However, he did not linger, as in the old days upriver, to talk and laugh with Leah.

That was how it was in the compound, slave men and their masters coming and going in the early mornings and late at night; this kept the household busy for most of the day and sometimes far into the night.

'I've known Will a long time, Sukie. He's never been one for women's gossip.'

'I'm not any woman so you can stop throwing words at me in that sly way you have. Will and I are together.'

'What do you mean, Sukie? Is Will your sweetheart? Tell me plain if that is what you are saying.'

Sukie bit her lips as though regretting her words. 'Not sweethearts, exactly. We're friends.'

'Oh, that's nice,' Leah said, her heartbeat slowing down. 'Will is friendly and good to people.'

'He wants me to meet him after the pit-pan races. He said it would make him paddle faster if he knew I was there cheering for him.'

'That's months away,' Leah said. 'But it's something for you to look forward to, I guess.'

'I'll send word to him upriver about how you are throwing words and bullying me.'

'All right, Sukie, you do that. I came by to see if all was well with you but I can see that it must be.'

Upstairs a bell was ringing vigorously but Sukie ignored it. She swished her broom across the floor making Leah step back to avoid the dust swirling in her direction. Her skirt brushed against shovels and paddles left leaning against a wall. They crashed to the ground.

The back door opened and the apothecary, Master Preston Dickey, a large white apron protecting his clothing, entered the shop looking around for the source of the noise. He was a heavy-set man with a protruding stomach.

'Sukie, your mistress is ringing her bell. Are you deaf now?'

He picked up the shovels and paddles and carried them to the back of the counter. His round face was red and his pale blue eyes with fair lashes seemed to bulge with annoyance. With an effort he controlled his anger, bowing briefly in Leah's direction.

Through the open doorway she saw his twin brother, Frederick Dickey, who ran their mahogany works upriver, leaning against the front wall of the laboratory where two slaves were stacking firewood for the brick oven. Mr Frederick Dickey had the same fair colouring as the apothecary but he was taller. The work upriver had made him broad about the chest. His tanned arms were muscled and he stood with one foot forward as though ready for a fight.

'I'm just going, sir,' Sukie said, throwing her broom to the ground.

'Well, get a move on.' The apothecary stood with his arms akimbo, glaring at her.

Leah watched Sukie climbing the curving mahogany stairs to the commodious floors above.

'The clerk will be here soon to open up,' the apothecary said. He indicated the wooden shutters, through which chinks of sunlight glinted on enormous blue and green glass bottles of varying sizes lining the back walls of the shop. 'May I help you with something, Mistress McGilvrey?'

Leah shook her head, slipping her shopping list into the side pocket of her dress.

'I came to visit my sister,' Leah said. 'I wanted to see how she was getting on.'

Master Preston Dickey shrugged his large shoulders.

'She peddles wares well so Mistress Caslow is prepared to keep her for the time being.'

'I see,' Leah said, listening to raised voices on the floor above. 'Thank you.'

The apothecary opened the screen door. He said good

morning as Leah walked out into the sunlight. She stood there for a minute allowing the wind from the sea to flow over her. To the right was a great mangrove swamp allocated by the magistrates for a new Government House. It was to be a wooden mansion facing the sea where future superintendents were to live.

Across the way was another site where the Anglican church was to be built, or so it was rumoured, with bricks brought from England; the bricks were used as ballast in the ships which arrived regularly to load mahogany, logwood and other valuable hardwoods.

To Leah the most interesting news was that people said the church was to start a school at some time in the future. She wondered if slave children would be able to attend. If it was true, then perhaps the church officials would accept her as a teacher to the youngest children. It was possible as she had been baptized. The Clare sisters were her godparents and she went to church at the Court House whenever Thomas was in town.

That last encounter with Sukie had happened several weeks before. Leah continued her slow progress along the Foreshore, squinting her eyes against the glittering sea on her left. She hoped that she'd get a chance to see Sukie privately and that she'd be in a better mood.

Chapter 25

In the distance Leah could see the sign of the mortar and pestle. A small crowd of people had gathered on the wharf opposite the apothecary's shop and residence. 'A master has probably died in the neighbourhood,' she thought to herself, wondering who it could be. She adjusted her straw hat, ridiculously small, perched on her circlet of black braids. She ran a finger under the tight elastic band at the base of her skull, holding the hat in place.

She wondered if Sukie had heard as yet about the abolition of the slave trade earlier that year. At the breakfast table some weeks ago, perhaps it had been at the beginning of the rainy season in late June, Thomas had read from the letter by his plate. He had raised his eyebrows, saying, 'The London agent writes that Parliament abolished the trade in March.' He tapped the packet of papers by his plate with his fingers, hairy above the knuckles. He glanced through the dining room door at the choppy sea foaming on the Foreshore.

'Oh my God,' Leah had said. 'The slaves are free now then, Thomas?' Hot black tea slopped over the rim of her cup, scalding her hand. She poured cold water from a jug onto a napkin and held it over the back of her hand, trying to soothe the burning sensation.

Was it really possible that the slaves were free or were about to be free? 'How odd,' she had thought to herself. If she'd waited, been less impatient, perhaps she would have been a free person in any case. Why this thought made her so uneasy, slightly ashamed and even disloyal, she could not have explained.

Leah looked across the table at Thomas, who was regarding her speculatively. She wondered if he had guessed some of what she was feeling. From her side of the large table, she could see the slave huts screened by a high hedge of hibiscus, its red, bell-shaped flowers lifting and falling in the squally wind. Berry, tall and skinny, the ends of her headscarf blowing against her face, was in the back yard to the rear of the stables Thomas had built. She was swiftly pulling the flapping bed sheets off the line. 'It will probably rain again soon,' she thought. 'I'll need to help Berry hang the rest of the laundry on the lines in the attic.' She hoped they would dry overnight as Thomas would need clean, ironed clothing for his return trip upriver in a day or so.

'The trade, the British trade,' Thomas was saying. 'No more slaves are to be bought or brought from Africa. I never thought I'd live to see it happen.' His eyebrows were drawn together and the lines on his cheeks seemed to deepen as he continued reading the letter.

'Oh,' Leah said, thinking of the manacled slaves loaded onto smaller boats from the slavers anchored beyond the reef. The harbour was too shallow for them to venture through the narrow channels in the barrier reefs. 'Who is to stop the crews from bringing slaves out from Africa?'

'The British Navy, I expect,' he said, shoving the papers to one side of the table. He lifted a slice of buttered toast, brought it to his mouth and then put it back on his plate.

'Are your slaves free now then?' Leah asked, so anxious to know that she braved the look of annoyance on Thomas's face. His tanned skin looked pale.

'No, they are not free,' he said. 'Only the trade has been abolished. Slaves will become even scarcer and more expensive, especially here where the men escape so often and the women have so few children.' He paused, sliding the plate of eggs to the other side of the table. 'Although God knows we treat them as well as we can, better than they would be treated elsewhere.' He looked at Leah, then blew his nose on his handkerchief.

'Make sure,' he said, 'that you let the women know that they are not free, not only those here in the compound but those we rent out in the town. We don't want false rumours getting about.'

'Will they ever be free?' Leah asked, watching Thomas as he shoved his packet of papers into the inner pocket of his jacket. He pushed back his chair and left the table as though he had just thought of something important and was in a hurry to get away.

At the door he turned and said, 'I expect they will, sooner or later, if the abolitionists have their way. I'm going down to the Court House now and later to the warehouses. Are the Clare sisters visiting today?'

'They were here yesterday,' Leah said, thinking of Miss Evelyn and Miss Roslyn, wondering why it was more difficult to talk to them as frankly as she had sometimes done in the past. They were just as curious about her life, just as eager to offer any assistance they could, but her circumstances had changed; there were things she could not confide in them or in anyone else really, not even Thomas.

He patted her shoulders and left the room. She heard his boots on the stairs, his voice calling for his horse and the clip clopping of the horse's hooves on the road.

She listened to the first raindrops on the roof and the sudden swooshing of the wind, as she rushed around the dining room and hall closing the verandah doors and the windows, tilting the blinds against the rain. The house was an easy one to live in and she took great pride in her housekeeping, doing things as carefully as she had seen them done in the home of the Angas brothers; she considered theirs to be the very nicest one in which she and her mother had worked. However, she did not feel entirely comfortable in any of the rooms which to her seemed haunted by Graham Lawson's dour presence.

She closed the door to the outside hallway and returned to sit at the table, thinking about what Thomas had said about the slave trade and remembering the last day she, Sam and Hannah had spent in the small room, attached to many others, under one roof in Eboe Town. The older she got, the more the memories of her youth surfaced in her mind, even as she tried to adjust to the pleasures and strictures of her present life as Thomas McGilvrey's wife.

Chapter 26

On that last day at Eboe Town, Leah, Hannah and Sam were sitting on the steps outside their old room. They were waiting for the mule and cart which would convey them with their few belongings to Thomas McGilvrey's compound. To keep their minds from contemplating the impending change, Leah was reading to them from *Robinson Crusoe*.

It was hard, though, to concentrate on Crusoe's man, Mr Friday, who they had concluded must be a slave. This part of the book was proving to be a bit troubling to them, as Sam kept wondering what would eventually happen to Mr Friday.

Leah still liked to read *Robinson Crusoe* because Crusoe's daily problems seemed as grave as their own. The story gave her courage and removed her from the realities of her own life. The book and the silk scarf, given to her by Josiah, were still her most treasured possessions, precious tokens from a time of youthful hopes and dreams. There was seldom a day in which her thoughts did not stray to Josiah. As the months went by, she wondered if a time would ever come when his memory would dissolve in her mind, like salt in warm water.

Leah did not like to think that her hurt and disappointment would last as long as she lived. However, she was beginning to suspect that he was now a part of her being, like an extra limb, or like a series of pictures which, at unexpected moments during the day, went round and round in her brain. It was often necessary to distract herself from these thoughts which made her feel ill or tearful.

She shuddered, feeling the chilly wind on her body. Goose bumps had formed on her bare arms and legs – she seemed to feel the tiny hairs rising as though to attention. Hannah was saying, 'He looks a bit on the cold side to me.' She held a rectangular bottle of coconut oil close to her thin chest. 'Though he's a good man, no doubt.'

'Who?' Leah asked, feeling slightly confused. She looked at her mother, who had now lost all of her front teeth. Her hair was so thin she could barely make two plaits to tuck behind her ears.

'Mr Thomas McGilvrey,' Hannah said, rubbing coconut oil onto Sam's face, arms and legs which were dry and ashy from the north wind which made them shiver as they huddled together on the rotting wooden steps.

'Why do you say that?' Leah asked, watching Sam biting his fingernails. She wrapped the book into her scarf and tucked it into her bundle. The scarf was the nicest thing she owned and she thought she might drape it over her head when she married Thomas McGilvrey. The service, to be carried out by the chaplain in the rectory office, was to be discreet and hurried. The chaplain, the Reverend Matthew Burke, was a taciturn individual: tall, with flowing blonde hair. His wife, Catherine, seemed friendlier. She was small and thin with black hair parted in the middle and twisted into a bun on her neck. 'Why do you think Mr McGilvrey is cold, Mama?' Leah asked again.

'I said he looks cold to me,' Hannah said. She was nervous, agitated, her face almost frightened.

'You mean, Mama, he's not friendly like the Clares or the Angas brothers?'

'I don't know what I mean,' Hannah said, wiping her oily palms over her own face. 'It's just hard for me to take in all at once, that's all.'

'It's been a long time since you lived in Graham Lawson's compound, Mama. He's dead now and can't hurt us any more. Things will be different for us, you'll see.'

'In my mind, things will always be the same, Leah, no matter what else changes for us. You can't know the sacrifices and bargains I made to get away with you and Sam, to keep you all safe, away from what I had to put up with from the time I was a girl.'

'I know it was a terrible time, Mama, but you have me and

Sam. You'll never again do anything you don't want to do. We love you so much,' Leah said, pulling her mother's head on her shoulder and stroking the burn scars on her right hand.

Sometimes when her mother changed her clothes in her presence, Leah saw a brand on her left shoulder. Leah had heard that branding used to be done, and probably still was, with a silver brand heated in spirits or wine, but her mother would never allow her to see it closely or to talk about when it was done or who had done it. 'Tell me about how it was when you were a girl, Mama. I need to know.'

'I can't go over all that, Leah. It would just about kill me to put those things into words. I feel ashamed of some of the things I had to do. If I start thinking of the days before in that compound, I don't think I could go with you and Sam. A lot of blood was spilt there, filling in the swamp, building that house and other things. It was the same all around for people like us.'

'I'm afraid too, Mama, about what is to come. But I need to take the risk. You always did whatever you had to do to protect us.'

'I know that's what you are doing, Leah. Once we are there, I'll be all right. But I never really believed it would happen, until now.'

They sat close together in the relative silence of the usually busy and noisy pathways of Eboe Town. Occasionally, from high up in a tamarind tree, a crow cawed and flapped its wings. Hannah coughed slightly as she inhaled smoke from a nearby cooking fire.

'Come back here, Sam,' she said, but Sam was again peering through the door of the empty room next door.

'Did you know that the lady and her baby were so hungry, Mama?' Sam asked. 'I heard the baby crying at night.'

'They didn't die from lack of food,' Hannah said. 'I often gave her some of what we had. Other people did too and she got her rations regularly from the McGilvrey agent, the same as we all do.'

'Why did they die then?' Sam asked. His eyes were riveted on the dirty bundle of bedding in the middle of the room.

'She didn't like living,' Hannah said, 'and neither did her baby, I expect.'

Leah saw that Sam was dissatisfied with Hannah's answer but he returned to the steps where they had been waiting for the cart since first light. Leah thought of the woman next door who had eaten dirt and fed it to her baby, until they became too sick to live. The thought of that hidden life going on behind the closed door and window of the room next door made her stomach heave and she leaned over, retching up the bread and tea she had eaten before dawn. Hannah had told her that the discovery the previous morning of the bodies of the woman and the baby clasped in her arms was a bad omen. Thomas McGilvrey had lost two valuable slaves.

She felt her mother rubbing her back and Sam touched her arm. 'The cart is coming, Leah,' he said. 'Try to hold up.'

Saliva was frothing from the mule's mouth and he whisked his tail to rid himself of flies which swarmed up from the dirt. The driver's face was hidden below his wide, fraying straw hat. He looked straight ahead, his scrawny arms and hands wrapped in the reins. He spat tobacco juice on the ground and growled at his mule.

People stood in their doorways staring curiously as Leah and Sam helped Hannah up beside the driver, who continued to look straight ahead. After they had thrown their bundles into the back of the cart, Leah and Sam climbed aboard. She looked curiously around the neighbourhood where she had spent most of her life. Already she felt like a stranger there. It was odd to think that she was returning to live in the compound where she had probably been conceived and although she would probably never know, taken her first steps and spoken her first words.

As she sat in the cart, rumbling along the rutted roadways, she made a resolution to help her mother to make a new start. She would not press her to talk about her childhood and girlhood as a slave in Graham Lawson's compound. She could guess well enough. Examples were everywhere and she looked about her as though she was seeing clearly, for the first time, the ways of the town in which she lived.

Chapter 27

These thoughts were uppermost in Leah's mind now as she smoothed the pleats of her dress made from fine white cotton. It had been freshly starched and ironed the day before but it was already drooping in the increasing humidity of mid-morning. She'd discovered long ago that she needed to walk at a moderate pace, dressed as she nearly always was these days in an array of wide skirts, hats and shoes which were not always comfortable. In the old days she'd sped in relative anonymity along the roads, by-ways and alleys at a speed unthinkable now.

She drew in a deep breath, inhaling the sweetish scent of body powder which smelt like Edmond after his morning and evening baths. She'd left him in the care of her mother, whose health, during the past year, had continued to improve. Hannah helped Leah to supervise the household and Miss Sheba, the cook, and Berry, her assistant, treated Edmond as though he was their own child.

From the beginning of their marriage, Leah, at Thomas's suggestion, had occasionally visited or discreetly enquired about the several female slaves who were rented out. Miss Sheba, Hannah or Berry accompanied her on the more difficult visits and were usually her witnesses when floggings, chaining to bedposts and the like had to be diplomatically dealt with.

Leah wished now that she'd left at home the silk parasol which she hardly ever used. It was a pretty, frivolous thing, with golden tassels on the curved handle. Sukie was bound to resent it. The parasol, a glowing cream colour in the sunshine, had been a gift from Thomas a few months after Edmond had been born on a stormy night in September in 1802. Twirling the parasol over her shoulder, she realized that, for some strange reason, it made her feel protected, less insecure, although why she'd felt she needed the parasol as a defence against Sukie, she wouldn't have liked to admit, even to herself.

Torrential rain had fallen after Edmond was born. She still remembered the sound of the rain against the window panes, the howling winds thrashing the palm trees and the croaking of the frogs in the soggy garden of the compound. Haulover Creek overflowed its banks and people paddled doreys through the flooded streets. Thomas had been at home for Edmond's birth and he'd looked down at the baby cradled in her arms and said, 'I thought he'd be darker, like you.' Thomas's face was red with pleasure but he looked a little puzzled as he stroked the baby's cheek.

'Are you disappointed in his looks?' Leah asked, amazed because until now Thomas had seemed to give little thought to the hierarchy of colour which obsessed settlers and slaves in the settlement.

'No, of course not,' Thomas said. 'Only his complexion is not too different from that of my poor first son.'

'He'll probably grow darker as he grows older,' Leah said. 'That's how it is, most of the time.'

'Not that it matters,' Thomas said, 'so long as he is healthy and strong. By the time he's old enough, I'll have that house built at Roaring Creek and then we can all be together during the dry season. Would you like that?'

'Yes,' Leah said, feeling anxiety stirring at the base of her spine. She tried not to think of those months upriver, carrying water from the well, chopping firewood and helping to clean gibnut, peccary, mountain cow and other game under the shade of sapodilla and mayflower trees, before the slaves had revolted. Unbidden, the memory of the youngest deaf-mute came to mind and she wondered whether he and his family had left the settlement, as Will had suggested they might do.

'You'll need to guard him against malaria,' Thomas said, lowering the voluminous mosquito net over Edmond and herself.

The baby had been named after a relative of Thomas's who for many years had been kind to him. Thomas's parents had died when he was quite small and this relative had cared for him until he was eleven. From that time until now he had usually made his own living in one way or another on the streets of various places like Edinburgh, Liverpool and London.

Thomas often claimed his life had been rougher and more brutal, in most ways, than Leah's had been. She seldom spoke to him now about the life she'd previously led in the settlement, for Thomas was sure to interrupt and tell her about his own youth when, so he said, he'd lived mostly on dry bread and weak beer for days at a time. To Leah it had begun to feel like an unfriendly competition, instead of a sympathetic conversation about the similarity, on opposite sides of the world, of their youthful experiences.

As Thomas tucked the mosquito netting in around the mattresses, Leah noticed how prosperous he looked of late in a fine cotton shirt with frills, brown jacket and trousers, silk stockings and black shoes with silver buckles which gleamed in the candlelight. Her labour had started shortly before he was to be ferried, in a canopied pit-pan, to a meeting of the magistrates at the Court House.

'What time is it?' Leah asked, looking down at her newborn son who was fast asleep. His fists were tightly closed and his mouth was puckered.

'After midnight,' Thomas said, looking at his gold watch which hung on a fine gold chain. 'Hannah said she'll sleep in here again tonight. Get some rest.'

'Are you leaving soon?' For some reason, Leah felt like weeping but she fought back the tears and swallowed hard to ease the tightness in her throat. Thomas didn't always handle emotion very well. He also seemed uncomfortable with the clutter and smells in the room.

'In a day or so, most likely. I've ordered boxes of machetes, axes, barrels of Irish pork, flour and so on. Once they're loaded, I'll need to get back upriver. I should soon be able to leave Horton in charge for longer periods.'

Roderick Horton, Thomas's new agent, was a barrel-chested older man with excessively long fingernails, who'd arrived from Jamaica over six months before.

'Do you like him?' Leah asked. She had met Horton about two or three times before he went upriver. Thomas had brought him to dinner twice. Each time Horton had looked at her with a knowing look in his bulging grey eyes, shiny from excessive wine. To her, Horton seemed to be saying, 'I've met your sort before. You don't fool me with your airs and graces.' On both occasions he'd pinched her cheek and patted her arm when Thomas was not looking.

'He's an all right enough fellow. Good company in the bush, especially at night when we're having a drink.' Thomas sighed. 'But he doesn't get on with the slaves out there very well. He tries to drive them like he's still on a Jamaican plantation.'

'It'll take him a long time to understand mahogany work. He might get hurt, if he's not careful,' Leah said, thinking about the small revolt in the bush which she and Sam had witnessed and remembering Buck, who had been beaten every day for a week until he died. She closed her eyes against the image of Will and Sharper swimming across the murky pond towards the caves where several runaway slaves had hauled them to safety.

'I've made Will captain of the slaves now. Together with Sharper and Sam, Will should be able to keep things under control until I get back. They send you their greetings, by the way. They'll be glad to know you are safely delivered of such a fine, healthy baby.'

'Give them my best wishes and my love to Sam. With all this rain, they'll be floating logs to Boom just about now, I imagine.'

'I need to get back, although it's tempting to stay and just watch baby Edmond.'

'No, of course, you mustn't stay,' Leah said, thinking of Will, Sharper and Sam driving the cattle-carts loaded down with mahogany to the riverside.

'Do you need anything?' Thomas asked, lighting another candle which made his shadow loom against the wall facing the bed. 'Shall I sing you to sleep?'

'Yes, please,' Leah said. She closed her eyes and drew Edmond closer, listening as he sang softly. No matter what he sang, his voice still enchanted her senses. Nevertheless, she was sorry he'd chosen 'Greensleeves' for it always made her want to cry. She lay still listening to the many verses he knew by heart. 'Such a beautiful voice, such a beautiful voice,' she thought to herself. He must have thought she was falling asleep for he lowered his voice singing very softly,

> *'Your vows you've broken like my heart,*
> *Oh why did you so enrapture me?*
> *Now I remain in a world apart*
> *But I remain in captivity.'*

After a few moments, he rose from the chair and tiptoed to the open door, closing it softly behind him. She heard his footsteps echoing along the hallway which led to his own room. There he would probably sit until nearly dawn, poring over his letters and charts. Perhaps he would open his travelling desk and take out the miniature picture of his first wife and place it on the vast rectangular table, amidst his plant and wood specimens. He had placed the table between two windows which looked out onto the wide verandah and the sea.

After she had lived with Thomas for a few months, Leah began to realize, by the things he asked her to do, that he had married her in part because he thought that this would raise his standing with the slaves. Thomas probably hoped he would have more credibility with them when they realized that he had married one of them. He had believed, Leah guessed, that runaways, suicides, slow-downs, murders, insanity and minor rebellions would become less frequent on his estate.

At meetings and dinners, the settlers complained incessantly about their loss of capital in slaves, their fear of slave revolts and the fact that they could not claim the land on which they were only allowed to cut mahogany through treaties signed by the British with Spain.

It was a wonder to Leah that, after all this time, she had not yet grown quite used to his self-absorption, nor had she yet gained much insight into his way of thinking about a great number of things which he took for granted. He had specific views on the furnishings in the house, the way the beds were to be made and her clothing, which he helped her to choose. He had a particular aversion to curtains, especially those with floral designs, and he would not have anything remotely resembling what he called 'oily doilies' anywhere in the house.

Her manumission paper and the marriage certificate, wrapped in cloth and sewn into a leather pouch which she strapped to her body every day, did not make her feel very different inside. It was a daily struggle to remind herself that she was no longer a slave and should not still feel like one or act like one. But it was not easy, particularly as Thomas was away for most of the year and she postponed many household decisions until he was home. The one great change in her life was the freedom and time in the evenings to read many of the books stacked against the walls in every room in the house.

The change in her status had caused the slaves she knew to dislike her, perhaps even despise her. It hurt to know that some of them laughed at her behind her back. The slaves did not believe she could, or would, do as much for them as a white woman would have done. Leah admitted to herself that in this last they were probably right. As a former slave, she did not have very much influence in the white settler community.

The only friends she could still count on were her mother, Sam and the Clare sisters. She was no longer quite so sure about Will and Sharper and this created a great void in her heart.

The room in which she lay with Edmond breathing gently against her cheek was the only one she had ever had in her life and she guarded it with a fierceness that continually surprised her. She would not allow any of the household slaves to clean the room, which was one of her greatest joys. When she was inside she bolted the door, and whenever she left she padlocked the door and carried the chain with the household keys on a brass ring which hung neatly amongst the folds of her dress. She decided to make another pouch for the keys because they made an annoying noise as she walked about the house or in the surrounding compound.

Her mind filled with the duties of the household which she performed with great energy and interest. It was the one way she could show Thomas how grateful she was for his kind ways, of which he had many – when he remembered or when things were brought to his notice.

On a table in one corner of the room was the leather-bound volume in which she had been writing the day before. It was her duty to keep the account book up to date, including the prices paid for steers, bulls, cows, slaves, horses, saddles, bridles, chains, yokes, oxbows, iron work, saws, machetes, pit-pans, doreys, book cases, chests of drawers, liquor cases, tea-boards, spyglasses, mattresses, bolsters, pillows, pictures, medicine chests, sofas, gold and silver buttons and buckles and other things which took up more than half the pages in the book. In another volume, she listed the slaves who had been sold, their prices and anything else for which payment had been received.

Edmond stirred beside her and Leah, putting a finger in his curled fist, raised it to her lips and pressed his little body against her chest. She thought about the changes in her life which had been beyond her imagining. She was busy from morning until night superintending the household affairs and didn't leave the compound very much. In a way, she felt less free than she'd been when she was a slave moving about the town – as an assistant laundress moving from one household to the other.

Now she was observed, gossiped about. Silences fell as she walked along. Older slaves like Will's friend Congo Jack were overly polite to her. The few young slaves in the town giggled behind their hands and some, of middling age, raked her from head to toe with envious eyes, evaluating her clothing, her shoes, her hat and her bags. On the streets, she tried to act as normally as she could but it was difficult to ignore the stares from kitchen windows, the hissing from yard-men and the occasional single slap of a drum as she passed by. The reaction of the slaves, some of them her former acquaintances, frightened her.

She tried to explain these feelings to the Clare sisters on their last visit as they'd sat on the verandah sewing, while Edmond played with the empty cotton reels the Clares had brought for him.

Miss Roslyn, in a figured muslin dress, had sipped on her sour-sop drink before replying, 'It'll take them a few years but people will get used to it.'

Miss Evelyn brushed the crumbs from a coconut tart off her black crepe skirt. Retrieving the needle and thread which she had pinned to the bosom of her dress, she said, 'I don't know about that, Roslyn. People don't forget. Look at you and me. We are sisters, mulattos people call us. Yet because I am the darker of the two of us, people treat me differently.' She scowled at her sister, as though challenging her to dispute that fact.

'I don't notice people treating us differently, Evelyn. You are too thin-skinned. In any case, we were talking about Leah.'

'Well, Leah is the darkest of the three of us, so she's bound to feel it in her present circumstances when people go out of their way to put her in her place.'

Leah smoothed out the small trousers she was altering for Edmond, who was already tall for his age. She continued unravelling the hems of the trousers as the Clare sisters argued animatedly about the hierarchy of colour in the settlement. It was late afternoon when they said goodbye, reminding Leah that it was her turn to visit them next.

Chapter 28

SUKIE

Early one morning in August, Sukie slipped through a side door of the apothecary's shop, almost hidden from view by the low-hanging branches of the plum trees bending over with ripened fruit. She picked one off the ground and rubbed it against her apron before popping the rust-coloured fruit into her mouth. She savoured the creaminess of the plum on her tongue as she climbed the stairs to the living quarters above the apothecary's shop.

As she spat the seed onto the ground below, she gave a quick glance sideways at the sign of the mortar and pestle swinging in the wind. Sukie gave a slight shudder thinking of the snake curling around the pestle on the sign. She hated snakes and wondered, as she did every day, why the snake had been painted in such a realistic way, with its fang showing through its mouth. She'd tried to find out about the snake but had never received a satisfactory explanation. She suspected it had something to do with the poisons locked away in the apothecary's shop.

She now knew a fair amount about the uses for certain herbs and medicines. She loved working in the shop but had soon discovered that she would never be allowed to touch the various medicine drawers about which she was so curious. 'Ah well,' she thought to herself, 'I'll just continue using my eyes and ears.'

Wiping her bare feet carefully on the mat, she pushed the door open and walked down the polished floorboards of the hallway to a workroom where Mistress Caslow, a very pale-brown-skinned woman, sat in her high-backed chair. She was selecting the items for sale from an iron-bound trunk. Sukie watched her warily, for she didn't want to anger Mistress Caslow or make an enemy of her. Once upon a time, Sukie knew, Orissa Caslow had been a proprietress of land, houses and slaves. She'd once been married.

It was said that during a period when she was gravely ill and thought herself near death, she had signed over all her property to her husband, who had sold everything and left the country with all the accumulated wealth of decades.

On the table beside Mistress Caslow was a pair of heavy scissors which she used to cut off the handkerchiefs from the packages piled up in the trunk. A neat pile of account books were in the middle of the table. She patted them with one small delicate hand as though she intended to prevent them from disappearing while her attention was elsewhere.

'Seventeen handkerchiefs are missing,' Mrs Caslow said, pushing strands of long, curly, reddish hair under the lace edges of her cap. 'Where are they?'

Sukie picked up the wooden tray from the floor and slipped the leather strap over her head. She was very frightened, for Mistress Caslow was not a person to be trifled with. 'I don't know, madam. I gave you the money for what I sold yesterday and brought the rest in here last evening. You saw me.' Sukie looked into the greenish eyes with long black lashes and wondered if it could be true that she practised obeah. People said that she used her knowledge to control her suitors – of which there had been a number – and her enemies.

'Do not call me madam. How many times do I have to tell you that?'

'Mistress Caslow, I swear mam, all the 'kerchiefs I didn't sell were on the tray when I placed it in here.'

'I've had everyone's things searched, including yours,' Orissa Caslow said, dabbing a muslin handkerchief with rose water and placing it over her nose. 'They are nowhere to be found and the money is short one doubloon.'

'Are you sure you counted right, Mistress Caslow?' Sukie asked, her heart racing. She'd tried so hard to do her best, peddling the handkerchiefs far and wide in the town. She wanted to stay at the apothecary's to learn the secrets of healing. When she did, she would have the power to earn money of her own in the town.

'I did count the money and the handkerchiefs many times. As far as I can gather, you were the last person to handle them,' Mistress Caslow said, rising to her feet, dainty in their embroidered slippers. She smoothed the folds of her striped black and white sateen frock which glowed in the light streaming into the window.

'Unless you tell me where they are, or what you did with the doubloon you received for them, I'll ask Mr Dickey to take you in hand.'

Sukie listened to the low voice, trying to detect any hint of softening in it, but she came to the conclusion that Mistress Orissa Caslow did not like her any better now than she had three years before. This thought made her very sad, for she had tried to model herself on this handsome woman who had been born free, just as Sukie believed herself to be.

'I don't know where they are Mistress Caslow,' Sukie said, her eyes filling with tears for she had wanted Mistress Caslow to like her, to explain to her the contents of the medicine chest in her commodious room overlooking the sea. When the wind blew through the windows, the room smelled of the orange and clove pomanders that Mistress Caslow had taught Sukie to make. The room, with its quilted bedspreads, drapes and mahogany dressing table and bureau, was Sukie's idea of paradise.

Her weekly visits there to help with the changing of the sheets and the re-spreading of the huge bed with its tall backboard were the high point of her week. To smell the hair pomade on the dressing table, the perfume bottles, to glimpse the silk and muslin gowns in the wardrobe, showed her a life that she knew she probably could have had, if only she'd been born beautiful, shapely – more womanly, like Mistress Caslow or Leah.

At one time Orissa Caslow had suggested that she might

allow Sukie to learn about the extensive assortment of drugs and chemicals in the warehouses. If she proved able, she would one day be able to help the clerk package family medicines and medicine chests; these were for those families obliged by peculiar circumstances to live in the bush and on the cayes beyond the reach of medical aid.

However, she had not learned to please Mistress Caslow, who said that she was tired of hearing reports about her from the other slaves. They complained that Sukie insisted she was descended from an Indian mother from the Miskito Shores and that she was not really a slave and shouldn't be forced to work like one.

Mistress Caslow had told Sukie time and again that whether or not she was a slave was none of Mistress Caslow's business. While she was in the apothecary's household, she should cease that kind of talk and save it for her master, who was now Thomas McGilvrey.

'If you insist on lying,' Mistress Caslow said now, 'please return downstairs. Tell Master Dickey that I said you are to be lashed and placed in the storeroom until I tell him otherwise.'

'Yes, mam,' Sukie said, tears streaming down her face. 'But I really don't know what happened to the handkerchiefs. I gave you the money for every one I sold.'

Later that same morning, Sukie was given ten hard lashes with the cat-o'-nine-tails by a strong woman slave. She spent the rest of that day in the redbrick storeroom adjacent to the outside laboratory. Evening came and lamps were lit in the house and in the shop. Shadows crept along the walls and tree branches scraped them. Sukie began to fear that giant rats would nibble at her toes or that a snake would uncoil itself from the rafters and drop onto her head.

She leaned against the bars of a window looking out into the moonlit yard. The redbrick storeroom was used for punishing recalcitrant slaves and to hold slaves newly arrived in the settlement and bought by the apothecary and his brother. After a few weeks the new slaves were usually taken upriver to work in the camps. There were iron rings set into the walls and chains were piled up in the corners. She stayed awake all night until early morning when she was given a mackerel and two ripe plantains to eat.

As she made an attempt to eat a part of the salted fish, she watched the early morning sunlight dappling the tree leaves which turned this way and that in the breeze. She remembered the first time she'd been accused of stealing. She and Leah had been young girls then, serving in the household of Mistress Dorinda and Master Basil Potts. Their cook had accused Sukie of stealing six of the hot powder buns for the family's tea, left to cool on a ledge outside the kitchen window.

The cook had chased her around the compound, whipping her legs and calling her a thief. Sukie bawled as loudly as she could, more from shame than from pain. She had called Leah's name and when she appeared, they had hidden themselves behind the tree-high red-bell bushes near to the wash-house where Leah had been assisting the laundress.

'Sukie,' Leah had said, 'did you take the buns? Tell cook if you did, then we'll stay together. Otherwise, she'll tell Master Potts to send you someplace else.'

'You doubt me, eh?' Sukie said, gripping Leah's wrists with her skinny hands.

'No, I don't, Sukie,' Leah said. 'Anybody could have taken those buns.'

'Even you,' Sukie said, feeling ashamed even as she said the words. She didn't want to leave the compound, where she and Leah were taken care of by the cook and where, in the evenings, they played hoop games, hide and seek and clapping games with the other slave children and with Master Josiah and a few of his friends.

'I didn't take those powder buns!' Leah said, her face angry, her eyes filling with tears. She got to her feet and wrenched open Sukie's fingers clasped tightly around her wrist. 'I didn't and you know it.'

'I can prove that I didn't take them,' Sukie said, wanting to delay Leah's departure. She was the only friend she now had in the world.

'How?' Leah asked and her frown disappeared. She looked curious, anxious. She sat cross-legged on the ground, playing with the ends of her long plaits.

'Just a minute,' Sukie said. 'You'll see.' She ran to the wash-house and returned carrying a tumbler of water. 'Give me a hair from your plait.'

'Take one of your own,' Leah said. 'I don't like that idea. Who knows what you'll do with it?'

'It has to be somebody else's hair or it won't work,' Sukie said, not knowing if this was true or not but wanting to involve Leah in some way. 'I won't obeah you with it.'

Leah eventually gave her a long strand of hair and Sukie removed a gold ring from her pocket. She heard Leah's quick intake of breath.

'Where did you get that?' Leah asked, looking at the sunshine glinting on what looked like a wedding ring.

'It was a gift,' Sukie said. 'It belonged to my mother. Someone gave it to me. She said it was from my mother.'

'Was your mother married then?' Leah asked. 'You never said that before.'

'She must have been,' Sukie said. 'Why else would someone give me the ring and say it was my mother's?'

'How am I to know, Sukie?' Leah asked.

Sukie remembered how she had slowly and carefully strung the ring onto the strand of Leah's hair. The shadows of the leaves had made patterns on Leah's face and her pale hands. Sukie held the ring over the water in the glass and said, 'By St Peter, by St Paul, did I steal any powder buns?' She chanted the words over and over, glancing up every now and then to see Leah staring fixedly at the ring held low in the glass, just above the water.

'See,' Sukie said. 'The hair didn't move so the ring didn't bump against the glass. Now do you believe me?'

Leah nodded but Sukie could see the doubtful look in her eyes. Sukie hadn't admitted to taking the buns and, as Leah had warned, she'd been sent away to household after household until she'd arrived at the apothecary's shop and residence where she had hoped to stay.

In the storehouse, Sukie felt the dried blood from the welts sticking to her blouse and her head ached as if it would burst wide open. She leaned her forehead against the bars of the window and heard the clanking of the chains on her ankles. She wept, not because of the silk handkerchiefs which she had not stolen nor sold. Her sorrow now was because of the warm powder buns, fragrant with vanilla and coconut milk, which she had taken from the ledge and had eaten. She'd taken the buns to her secret corner to the rear of the wash-house, shaded by an enormous almond tree. The sun didn't reach the ground there and it was always cool and damp. Crabs had peered at her from deep holes in the mud and mosquitoes had buzzed around her face. After finishing the buns, she'd felt slightly sick and sorry.

A few weeks later, she'd been parted from Leah and, although the golden wedding ring hadn't bounced against the glass, Leah had guessed in the end that Sukie had taken the buns. She'd seen that knowledge in Leah's eyes as she'd gone back to work. Sukie had sat quite still for a few minutes looking down at the ring on the strand of Leah's hair and at the glass of clear rain water. She'd slowly climbed the back stairs to the kitchen, reluctant to face cook's angry face, astonished to discover that she now disliked Leah. She had done so ever since.

Later that day Sukie was led from the storeroom into the yard, chained to a tree and made to wash bowl after large bowl of laundry in the boiling hot sun. At various times during that day she was questioned closely by the apothecary and his assistant. When she continued to deny that she had stolen the handkerchiefs, the apothecary, red-faced and morose, said, 'I'll give you one more night to think about what you did with those handkerchiefs or the money. If you don't confess, you know what will happen.'

'I'd rather lose my head than confess to something I didn't do,' Sukie said.

She felt the blood caked on her back and neck from the wounds inflicted the day before. Flies buzzed around her and she knew that the cuts would soon fester. Sukie leaned back her head and laughed out loud, then quickly stopped, not wanting the watching slaves to think she was losing her mind. But she found it funny to think that she was only yards away from the apothecary's shop where, if she had access to it, she could begin curing her cuts with alcohol and salves.

She mourned the fact that all that was probably beyond her reach now. The knowledge of the horrors to come seemed as nothing compared with the knowledge that she had, almost certainly, lost her place at the apothecary's shop and her visits to Mistress Caslow's beautiful room. Most of all she thought she'd miss the pictures on the walls of beautiful women in curled white wigs, painted faces and elaborate dresses.

Chapter 29

The crowd of people milling around the apothecary's shop seemed to be growing larger. Leah closed her parasol and increased her pace. Slipping into the crowd, she edged her way along the white picket fence until she was at the gate to the open yard where the apothecary and his brothers were seated in chairs under the shelter of a spreading tamarind tree. Leah's heart skipped a beat as she heard loud screams from the storehouse.

Two male slaves dragged Sukie out into the open. 'Murder, they're murdering me,' she shouted.

The chains on her manacled legs were removed. The men tied her to the ground face down. Her arms and legs were stretched out and secured with cords to four stakes. She lay exposed in a perfect state of nature. The crowd murmured and counted until she was severely flogged thirty-nine times. There were women and men on the street, on the pier and on the verandahs of nearby houses. Others peered through kitchen windows and watched from the slave quarters to the rear of the house.

Leah opened the gate and climbed the front steps to the verandah. Mistress Orissa Caslow, clutching a shawl around her shoulders, was leaning over the railing looking down into the yard where Sukie was screaming in agony as salt was poured into her bleeding wounds.

'Mistress Caslow,' Leah said, raising her voice.

Orissa Caslow turned around, her face rigid with annoyance. 'Who invited you up here? What do you want?'

'Shame on you, Mistress Caslow, for allowing Mr Dickey and his brother to have Sukie beaten like this in public.'

'She was very insolent to me. She tore my gown and tried to throw me to the ground. I did my best to save her from this. She was confined in the store for days with only a very small chain fastened to her foot and still she didn't confess to selling the handkerchiefs and keeping the money.'

'I don't really intend to argue with you, Mistress Caslow. All I want is to have your permission to remove Sukie from these premises.'

'I'll be glad to be rid of her. But I won't release her until I get the doubloon I am owed.'

'You owe Mr McGilvrey for several months rental so if she leaves today, you won't lose.'

'On whose authority?' she asked.

'On mine,' Leah said. 'I am prepared to sign a receipt to that effect.'

'In that case,' Mistress Caslow said, 'come inside.' They entered the parlour. As Leah waited on a hard upright mahogany settee, Mrs Caslow left the room. A few minutes later she returned with Sukie's release written on a sheet of paper. Leah read it and signed her name.

Leah followed her down the stairs to the apothecary's shop. Orissa Caslow crossed to the screen door and called to Master Dickey. Leah turned her back as they whispered together at the door.

'Come with me,' Orissa Caslow said, leading the way to the slave quarters. 'You can wait for her here. I hope we will meet again under better circumstances, Mistress McGilvrey.'

Leah did not reply. She sat on a stool outside the door of the thatched hut which Sukie shared with other women slaves. After a while, Leah watched the crowd drifting away as Sukie was released and led towards the rear of the compound.

Blood streamed from the cuts on her body but she had stopped screaming. She wrenched her arms from the men who were holding her. Her hair was matted and she walked bent over, her arms crossed over her breasts. When she saw Leah, she gave a little shriek and dashed into the hut. Leah heard her stifled moans and saw her huddled on the dirt floor in a corner of the room.

A slave woman brought a bucket of water to the door of the room. Leah took it from her, unhooked a calabash from the outside wall and called, 'I'm coming in there, Sukie.' There was no answer. Leah entered the small, stuffy room. 'You are not to work here any more. They'll kill you if you get another beating tomorrow. I signed a receipt for your release.'

'Thank you for nothing,' Sukie said, 'I don't want to go anywhere else.' She drew a cloth from her bundle and wiped the blood from her face. 'I like working in the shop.'

'But they'll torture you until you tell them what happened to those handkerchiefs.'

'I didn't steal them,' Sukie said, dipping the cloth into the bucket of water. 'I prefer them to put me in the Court House prison or hang me but I'm not going to say I did when I didn't.'

'Then you'll die, bit by bit,' Leah said. 'You certainly won't be allowed back into that shop.'

'It'll be the same whoever rents me,' Sukie said. 'Everyone has some fault to find.'

'You won't ever be rented out again, Sukie. You can live and work in our compound. I promise.'

'Oh, so you are Miss High and Mighty now. What will the master say?'

'He will agree with me.'

'You signed that paper. You didn't ask me. I have no choice.'

'I'll wait for you outside,' Leah said.

'My face is all swollen and there's a cut over my eye. I'm not going out there like this.'

'We'll take a mule and cart,' Leah said.

After Sukie had washed and dressed, they sat together watching the sun sink behind the coconut trees. The lamps were lit in the apothecary's upstairs residence. The shadows of Mistress Caslow and the two brothers showed through the curtained windows. Plates and cutlery rattled. The smell of frying meat permeated the air. The cook's voice was raised in song. The gardener removed the stakes from the ground and they heard the dragging of Sukie's chains as he approached the storeroom.

They walked to the gate. Sukie leaned against the fence, her back to the street. Tears were in her eyes as she gazed fixedly at the blue and green bottles lining the front windows of the apothecary's shop.

Chapter 30

AUGUST 1813

That Sunday afternoon Leah rose from her worktable drenched in sweat. She crossed the room to one of the barricaded windows and peered at the sea receding into the far horizon. Unlocking her door she ran quickly to the verandah and then down the front steps to the Foreshore.

Townspeople were far out on the seabed. They were gathering the glittering fishes flapping about in the mud and sand.

Edmond, a tall sturdy boy, was shovelling sand into high mounds. Every now and then he stopped to stare at his father and Will, who stood with a group of settlers and slaves pointing out to sea. After a while, Thomas and Will walked to where Leah and Edmond stood waiting for them.

'Is it time to leave now, Papa?' Edmond asked, sticking his shovel into the wet muddy sand. He wiped his face with his sleeves, then wiped his hands on his trousers.

Leah kept her eyes on Thomas's lips, which twitched slightly as they did whenever he was nervous. His face had paled under his tan.

'Right away,' Thomas said. 'Tell the others and get yourself ready.' He drew Edmond towards him and brushed the sand from his hair. 'Hurry up now,' Thomas said, giving Edmond a little push.

'People feel sure it's a hurricane,' Thomas said to Leah. He put his arm around her shoulder. 'There's still time to get away.' He turned to Will. 'Are the pit-pans ready?'

Will nodded, his face tired and anxious. 'Sharper is sending the carts.'

'Good,' Thomas said, 'I was hoping it wouldn't be more than a bad storm.' He squinted at the glimmering sea many yards away.

Leah nodded but didn't say anything. There was little point

in reminding him that Hannah, Miss Sheba and even Berry had been talking all day about the approaching bad weather. Everyone was frightened by the glaring sunlight and the lack of air which seemed to have gone with the receding sea.

She hurried up the back stairs to the kitchen. Bundles and baskets were piled on the floor and on the scrubbed kitchen table. 'It's time to go,' she called. 'We are to take everything to the gate. The carts are coming in a minute. Where's Sukie?'

'She's collecting her belongings in the back, I think,' Miss Sheba said.

'Sukie, Sukie,' Leah called, running down the steps and to the rear of the house. 'Hurry up. It's time to get going.'

'I'm here, Leah,' Sukie said, emerging from the hut Will shared with Sharper when they were in town. She dragged two bundles through the door and deposited them next to Leah's. 'I know it's time to go. Will and Sharper gave us warning since early morning.'

Leah drew in a deep breath, feeling a stitch in her left side. She held her hand against it, waiting for the pain to pass. She ignored Sukie's reproachful face, picked up one of the bundles and walked towards the gate where a mule and cart had drawn up.

Sukie gave a nervous laugh and then said, 'That's Will's bundle, you know.'

'Really?' Leah said. 'What of it?'

Sukie laughed.

To Leah, the sound was more like a cackle and grated on her nerves. She dropped the bundle near Sukie's feet and returned upstairs.

Thomas was in his room wrapping up his personal papers in tarpaulin, tying the packages expertly with cord.

'Let's see if this will work,' he said, as Leah entered the room. 'Put your hands through the loops. How is that? Not too heavy?'

'Not too heavy,' Leah said, looking around the room at the

boxes of specimens, papers, books and pictures which were to remain behind with most of their household effects.

The room darkened and they both moved to the barred windows to peer out at the sea frothing in the distance.

'I think it's on the turn,' Thomas said. 'We'll be inundated. Everything will be lost.' He pressed her closely to him and kissed her forehead.

The town was below sea level and the surge could rise above the trees and the houses. It seemed to Leah that she could almost see the houses and huts dashed into the sea.

There were many people, like Thomas, who had decided to remain in the town. She felt the cords of the package digging into her shoulders.

'Thomas,' she said.

'Mmm?' he said, putting memorandum books, quills, pen knives and new candles into two leather fire buckets.

'When the surge comes in, there'll be little you can do here.' Leah said. 'We need you to come upriver with us.'

'Not afraid, are you?'

'Yes,' Leah said, 'I'm afraid for you staying here.'

From a cupboard he removed an iron chest in which he kept various denominations of money, common pistols, silver watches, a gold chain and several packs of playing cards.

'I prefer to weather it out here,' he said, 'to reduce our losses as best I can, especially at the warehouses. I want you to put a tarpaulin over this chest and sit on it, if you can.'

'All right,' Leah said, looking at his face, which appeared drained. He gestured to the package on her back.

'Try to keep that safe. I'm depending on you now. Keep watch on the trunk until I get upriver.'

'Yes,' Leah said, 'I'll be careful.'

'Another thing,' Thomas said. 'Roderick Horton is planning to stay in the settlement. He wants to purchase a few slaves from me so that he can get his own mahogany concession.'

'Oh?' Leah said, wondering why Thomas had chosen this moment to tell her about Horton's plans. She knew he cared for Horton as little as she did.

'He wants to purchase Sukie. He'll probably mention it when you see him.'

'Why don't we wait to see what will happen? If the hurricane is very bad, people are going to die. Some of the slaves will go over the border.'

'You may be right,' Thomas said, 'but I don't want you to be surprised. He might mention it to you.'

'I'll tell him to discuss it with you,' Leah said.

He hugged her and they promised each other to be careful. 'Keep Edmond at home until I get there,' Thomas said. 'No wandering off with Will or the cattlemen.'

'We'll both stay close to the house until you reach us.' They heard Edmond calling to them from the street.

'I'll go with you to the creek to see that you get off in good order,' Thomas said. 'It'll be a rough trip. The creek is crowded with boats.'

As they walked through the house, Leah thought of all that would be washed away. She would miss the dining table, looking glasses, mahogany chairs, silver tumblers and a variety of other things in which they'd taken such pleasure.

In her purse she had twelve silver tea spoons, five silver thimbles, her silk scarf and *Robinson Crusoe*. She had started reading it again yesterday, realizing with a slight shock how many of the details had faded from her memory. The scene in which he battled the waves, holding on until eventually he lay exhausted on the island sands, was vivid in her mind.

In about one hour, Leah, Edmond, Sukie, Berry and Miss Sheba were seated under the wide canvas awning of the pit-pan. Leah sat on the iron chest. She tried to make herself comfortable but the package Thomas had asked her to carry on her back was beginning to feel heavier and heavier.

Will and Sharper were directing the loading of the packages and bundles into various parts of the boat. At the creek-side, Thomas gave instructions and talked to them until the dozen or so slaves dipped their paddles into the water and they were off. Edmond stared at his father until they were far up the creek and the figure of Thomas waving his hat was no longer visible. Leah grasped Edmond's hand and squeezed it hard. He smiled and said, 'Don't worry, Mama, he'll be all right.'

'I know he will,' Leah said. She was tempted to remove the package from her back but she knew she wouldn't. Amongst the bulky papers she suspected that Thomas had added his greatest treasure, the miniature painting of his first wife Maryanne. She wondered what that slender, smiling woman would think if she could know that her painting was travelling upriver in a storm. 'I can bear it,' Leah said to herself. 'It's a small return.' She looked down at the swirling creek, concentrating on the strong dip and lift of the paddles.

Chapter 31

By late afternoon, the sky began to darken, the wind intensified and rain began to fall heavily. Leah prayed that they would not get a direct strike from the hurricane and that Thomas would find a high rooftop or tree, if the sea surge was as extreme as everyone feared it would be.

If that happened, the life they'd known during the past few years would disappear. It would take the settlers years to recover. Many settlers would never regain their losses.

She thought of the Clare sisters and of the Angas brothers. She added prayers for their safety and wondered if she'd ever see them again. Leah felt sure that they had all fled the town for they had connections at the numerous mahogany works, banks and camps up and down the rivers and creeks.

Even if the hurricane changed course, there would still be flooding, landslides and catastrophic damage along the coast and far inland.

Will was in the front of the pit-pan, watching the creek, making sure the paddlers steered clear of the other boats. As it grew dark, he lit hurricane lanterns and passed one back to the stern. The wind had begun to thrash the trees lining the river. Except for the occasional voices of the paddlers calling back and forth to each other, the others in the boat were silent.

They used sheets of tarpaulin to shield themselves from the worst of the wind and rain. Leah kept her eyes on Edmond, staring in awe at the turmoil in the creek, and the trees and bushes bending low over the water. She considered for a while how different Edmond's life was from the one she and Sam had led, scavenging for food in the creek during that Christmas season long ago. That was the first time she'd spoken to Thomas and heard him sing.

She'd be glad to see Sam again. She'd asked Thomas to grant

Sam's manumission later in the year, perhaps at Christmas time, and he had agreed. In spite of the losses they were bound to sustain, she felt sure he would keep his promise. Thomas had no fear that Sam would run away to the slaves hiding in the bushes and the limestone caves or try to find his way to the Spanish border. Sam was very close to Hannah, Leah and Edmond. He'd taught Edmond everything he knew about the bush.

The hours seemed to pass very slowly. They'd left the creek long ago and were now on the River Belize. A few trees had crashed into the water and time was lost pushing them out of their path. Hearing a triumphant shout from the paddlers, Leah peered over the tarpaulin to see the men steering off the river into Roaring Creek.

Soon they were nearing McGilvrey's bank and she saw lights in two of the huts. They drew alongshore and some of the men helped to lift them out of the boat onto the muddy ground. It was very slippery and their feet squelched in the mud.

Will had his arms around Sukie and Edmond, holding them close, trying to shield them from the wind and rain. They struggled to reach the hut. Sharper and a few of the paddlers helped Leah and the others as they climbed the hill.

A shout came from one of the huts. It was Sam who hurried out to them. He lifted Hannah into his arms and carried her into the hut. The agent, Roderick Horton, followed with a number of the cattlemen and other slaves.

In the house, the women sank down onto the floor, exhausted but grateful to the paddlers for getting them safely to high ground. After a while, they drank hot bush tea and ate the hard biscuits which the men gave to them. Leah eased the package from her aching shoulders and looked at Will, who nodded.

He called to Sharper and they quietly left the hut, struggling through the storm to the pit-pan at the creek-side. It was with great relief that Leah heard them returning, after what seemed like a long time, carrying Thomas's iron chest. It was only now that she felt the tension in her body ease.

'Is everyone in from the bush?' Leah asked, taking a tally of the people in the room.

'Everyone that's coming is in the compound,' Horton said. 'The others are making their way upriver to the Spanish border by now, I expect. We won't know for sure until the storm lets up.' He shook his head and said, 'We're in for several bad seasons with so few hands to log the forests.'

Chapter 32

During the next few days, Leah helped to settle everyone into the rambling house built on stilts by Thomas McGilvrey. They expected him to arrive at any time.

Edmond had a room next to Leah's in the front of the house. Hannah and Sukie had rooms on the other side of the corridor which ran down the middle of the house. Every day and during the night, someone walked down to the creek on the hour to look out for Thomas's pit-pan or some other craft bringing him to Roaring Creek. They'd heard news that the hurricane had completely destroyed the settlement and the water had risen over the rooftops. However, there was no word from Thomas.

The house was not far from a small waterfall which dropped into the creek. The sound of flowing water filled the house, which was surrounded by high fence posts that Thomas hoped would someday grow into shady gumbolimbo trees. The rain stopped and their outdoor activities began once again.

They cooked on the fire-hearth and ate together at a long table under the arching trees, smelling the comforting scent of wood-smoke which helped to keep the mosquitoes at bay. They slept under mosquito nets. Sometimes at night there were fireflies on the ceiling. Most nights Leah was unable to sleep before dawn. She listened to the neighing horses, the braying mules and the lowing cattle, waiting for someone to say that Thomas had arrived.

To the rear was a separate hut for Roderick Horton. There were also a number of other huts where Will, Sharper and the other slaves lived when they were not in the bush.

One evening, Hannah and Leah sat on the verandah husking corn. Sukie was carrying water from the well for the barrels lined up against the cookhouse. It had been seven days since they'd left town and Thomas had still not returned.

'I'm sure he is all right,' Hannah said, examining the silken hair from an ear of corn.

'Yes,' Leah said, keeping her eyes on Edmond, who was trying to catch hold of the wings of a needle-case fly which had perched on one of the clothes lines.

'No news is good news, so people say.'

'Yes,' Leah said, picking up a broom. She started to sweep up the corn silk and husks from the verandah floor. She called to Edmond, 'Time for your bath, come inside.' There was no reply so Leah turned to call again, but Edmond was running downhill crying, 'He's here, he's here.'

Leah stood at the door, feeling her heart thud as she saw four men carrying Thomas on a litter. Edmond was shouting, 'Papa, Papa, what's the matter?'

She waited at the door until the litter was brought nearer the verandah. Edmond ran behind, tears streaming down his face. 'Papa is sick,' he called, 'Papa is sick.'

Leah looked down at Thomas. His hair was matted, his face grey, his eyes closed. She laid a hand on his forehead. He was burning with fever.

The men carried the litter carefully up the twelve steps to the verandah, through the double doors and down the hallway. Leah pointed to a large room on the right. Inside they lifted Thomas, fully clothed, onto the smooth white sheets on his large double bed. Leah adjusted a pillow beneath his head and looked down at his trembling body. 'It's probably malaria,' she thought to herself.

Drawing the covers up to his chin, she said to the boatmen, 'Thank you. The agent, Master Horton, will return soon.'

She said to Edmond, who was gazing down at his father, 'Please help the boatmen to get their food, Edmond, and open one of the empty huts so they can rest.'

'Yes, Mama,' he said, wiping his face with the tail of his shirt.

Together they looked down at Thomas's restless body and

listened as he groaned. In the compound, someone was splitting wood for the fire-hearth.

'And tell them to stop that noise,' Leah said, as Edmond moved slowly away from his father's bedside.

'Thank you,' she said to the exhausted boatmen, who still seemed dazed as they glanced at Thomas's worktable. In the middle of it was his package still wrapped in tarpaulin and tied with string. Beside it was a clay water pot stuffed with the leaves of sorosi vine, the thorny wild pineapple and the negrito. Thomas enjoyed examining new plant specimens which he sometimes sketched and described in his journals.

She removed his boots, stockings and neckerchief as she waited for Hannah, who was boiling leaves from the fiddlewood tree. A bar of sunshine flickered across Thomas's face and he opened his eyes. 'Maryanne?' he asked, looking at Leah. 'Maryanne?'

'I'm here, Thomas,' Leah said, keeping her voice low, hoping it would somehow comfort him. She grasped his hands and re-settled his head on the pillow. His delirium caused her great alarm and agitation. She wondered how long he'd suffered with the fever. If it was malaria, there was no way of predicting whether or not he would recover.

Hannah entered the room with a pan of hot water and clean towels. 'Close those blinds. I'm going to wash him down.'

Leah helped to undress Thomas, whose skin felt hot and papery. He'd lost weight and his torn, muddy clothing hung loosely on his body.

He opened his eyes and raised a hand slowly to his unshaven face. 'Ah,' he said, letting his hand drop onto the covers.

Leah felt the hot tears on her cheek and released his hand. She helped her mother to turn him over, watching as Hannah carefully sponged and dried his body.

'Go outside and beat some of the scoggineal leaves for his head.' Leah went downstairs to the cactus plants growing beside the back steps. She cut, peeled and sliced a few of the thick green pads. With a mallet she pounded the leaves until the white insides were slimy. Putting the pulp into a clean cloth, she returned to the bedroom and watched as Hannah tied it carefully around his head.

They stayed with Thomas all that night, giving him sponge baths, water and tea brewed from the leaves of the jackass bitters plant. The following day, when he had not regained consciousness, it was clear to them that the fever had gone to his brain. By evening Thomas McGilvrey died without ever regaining consciousness.

Leah placed the small painting of Maryanne against his heart before they buried him under a guanacaste tree. He'd often patted the tree saying, 'The loggers left this alone because the trunk is divided naturally into so many sections.'

The tree was covered with orchids and vines of various kinds. 'No,' Leah had said. 'You couldn't even make a pit-pan or anything out of it.'

'Quite right,' Thomas said, 'lucky tree. It'll probably be here long after we're all gone.'

'Well,' Leah thought, listening to Roderick Horton reading from the prayer book, 'as long as the guanacaste lives, you'll be here in spirit, Thomas.'

Chapter 33

At Roaring Creek, Leah sat very quietly looking at the silhouette of a papaya tree against the whitewashed wall of her room. She was listening to the night sounds and to the beating of her heart. Except for Sam keeping watch on the verandah, the house and compound had been almost abandoned. For the first time, she felt glad that her mother was no longer able to clearly differentiate the present from the past.

She sniffed the breeze blowing through the window but she could not detect any scent of burning thatch. This didn't surprise her as she didn't think, in spite of everything, that Will and Sharper would want to kill her. Or would they? She was not close to them any more and it had been a long time since she and Will had spoken.

Leah stretched out one hand to turn down the oil lamp which stood on a small round table close to her mahogany bed. It was unlikely now that the superintendent of the settlement and the West India regiment would arrive that night. She and Sam would continue to keep watch until morning.

Through the window blinds she peered up at the full moon then glanced down at *Robinson Crusoe*. The moonlight was bright enough to read by but she closed the book. She gripped it tightly against her chest, trying to stop her fingers from shaking.

A considerable number of slaves, led by Will and Sharper, had formed themselves into a body on the River Belize and the River Sibun. The revolt had started slowly on 20 April and spread to other mahogany camps up and down the rivers and creeks. She'd heard that they were well-armed. As far as she knew, the animosity of the slaves had not led them into any great excesses and she prayed that this would continue to be the case.

She had been so busy during the years following Thomas' death that it was only now, in this crisis, that she had really begun to mourn his passing. She had not been conscious of missing him in the day-to-day running of the estate, which had been fraught with difficulties. She had at first felt exhilarated, challenged by her relative freedom to run the estate along the lines which Thomas had laid down. Bit by bit, she had instituted changes of her own, some of which were successful. Others had brought disaster into their lives.

Up to a week ago when, in haste and secrecy, she had paid a poor white settler to spirit her son to Belize Town, she had considered herself self-sufficient in her personal and business affairs. With any luck, Edmond was now on a ship scheduled to sail in a day or two for Scotland. She wondered whether his father's relations would be pleased to see Edmond arrive on their doorstep without prior warning.

While going through Thomas's letters, she had found the address in Glasgow. His cheque book showed that he had, over the years, remitted thousands of pounds to relatives he'd hoped never to see again. At least that's what he'd said. However, she was beginning to wonder if he'd been entirely truthful. It would have been a commonplace story. Many men, wealthy and free, regardless of colour, sailed to Europe or to America and were never heard of again.

Leah thought of Thomas's grave under the guanacaste tree. She wondered what he would have done in the present crisis. She had inherited his estate and all the people connected to it. It was rumoured that she'd used obeah to cast a spell on him.

Thomas would have laughed at this gossip. Then he probably would have looked at her slyly and said, 'Did you? I've often wondered what you learned from the obeah men and women in that slave yard in Eboe Town.' His inborn sense of superiority was often wearying and hurtful.

During their marriage, Leah had eventually admitted to herself that there were aspects of Thomas' character that were hidden from her. Every now and then he said or did something that showed he had certain assumptions about her and everyone like her. Whenever he discovered that he'd been mistaken about certain aspects of her character, he never admitted to it freely or in argument. Instead he would narrow his eyes and laugh in a way Leah sometimes felt was mean-spirited. He often got his own back in one way or another.

Once when Thomas had been drinking, he'd said, 'If you outlive me Leah, I do believe you'd run this place into the ground out of sheer malice.'

'Why do you say that?' she asked, wondering what had provoked him now.

'You give goods and money to anybody who asks. I don't believe you understand the value of money in the wider world and what I mean to do with it.'

'You can do what you like with your goods and money,' Leah had said. 'I only give to help your interests.'

These exchanges had often led to quarrels and, as self-protection, Leah said less and less until their conversations had dwindled to only what was necessary.

During the last year of his life, Thomas talked more and more about money. It had been difficult for her to understand his anxiety, as the logging seasons had been profitable for everyone before the last hurricane struck.

Every now and then Thomas talked about wanting to travel, to find the true source of the River Belize and to climb the mountains in the interior. From his papers she'd learned that he'd been planning an expedition to explore some of the nearby Maya ruins in which colossal trees grew. In his journal he'd written about a man he'd met who'd cleared away the bushes and excavated treasures from rooms in one of these ruins. Leah wondered now if

Thomas only dreamed of these journeys, whether he'd really planned to go and whether he would have returned.

She looked out on the compound drenched in moonlight. She thought of the jaguars and pumas prowling the forests and of the caves where escaping slaves hid during the daytime. She sighed. Over the years, she and Thomas had not grown any closer in thought. She'd not been able to cater to his many assumptions, especially once she'd discovered what some of them were.

Still, in spite of their differences, she'd liked him and had been grateful to him for shelter and protection. If he'd lived, Edmond would probably have been very different. He'd loved his father and Thomas' death had unleashed in Edmond a foolhardiness she had scarcely thought possible.

Chapter 34

Earlier that day Sam returned from the river and said, 'We've lost more than a dozen cattle and the provision grounds were raided.' He removed his straw hat and hung it on a hook behind the door.

'No reports of anyone else killed?' Leah asked, fearful of his reply.

'No,' Sam said, giving her a hard look. He sat down on a chair, his arms on his knees, his hands hanging down.

He looked through the door at the path which led down to the creek. The afternoon sun was shining and white clouds floated across the blue sky. The short curtains at the windows lifted gently when the wind blew, bringing indoors the fragrance of ripening mangoes and the scent of wine from the cashews rotting underneath the trees.

Leah gazed at her brother but he wouldn't meet her eyes. He was still very angry with her, disappointed that she had demoted Will and promoted Edmond. Will had been like an older brother and father to Sam and Edmond.

'I wasn't to know this would happen – that Will would be so upset,' Leah said. 'I did it to please Edmond, to give him something to do, to keep him at home.'

He looked at her and, feeling embarrassed, Leah said, 'I know he was angry that I sold Sukie to Roderick Horton. But he did free her and intends to marry her. He told me so.' She thought of Sukie's words when she'd learnt of her sale to Horton: 'I know why you are selling me, Leah. But you are going to regret it. I'll kill myself before I marry Horton.'

'He's agreed to set you free,' Leah said, her voice raised in annoyance.

'He won't free me unless I promise to marry him, to put my mark on a piece of paper. I know him.'

The front room seemed shadowed as the clouds moved

across the sun. She heard the distant howl of monkeys in the fig trees by the creek.

'Why didn't you talk to me, first?' Sam asked. 'I could have told you that Will and Sukie were sweethearts.'

Leah hung her head. She had no reply that she wanted to make to Sam.

'Or did you already guess?' Sam asked. 'I can't believe that you would hurt Will in that way. I didn't know you had such a jealous nature.'

Leah examined her fingernails closely. She had been appalled to discover the depth of her enmity towards Sukie. Will had been her special friend. She had felt devastated when Will asked her for permission to build a hut for Sukie and himself on the compound.

Sam rose from his chair and removed his hat from the hook behind the door. Twirling the hat in his hands he said, 'You could have put me in charge instead of Edmond. He is as cruel as Roderick Horton or any of the others.'

'Well, he's gone now,' Leah said. 'I doubt if he'll ever return here.'

'He'll be a dead man if he does,' Sam said. 'Our people won't forget the way he flogged Will and Sharper, who were his friends and taught him everything he knew.'

'I can't imagine what got into him,' Leah said, feeling her heart beat faster.

After Thomas died, Edmond had begun to emulate Roderick Horton and to look on him almost like a father. Edmond had chosen to obey Horton, to be led by him into drunken orgies, depravity and flagrant acts of cruelty.

'There are rumours that Edmond flogged a slave to death,' Sam said. 'Do you know who it was?'

Leah shook her head. 'I've heard that Edmond was drinking and carousing regularly at logging camps upriver and down but I don't believe he has it in him to kill anyone.'

'Did you ask him outright?' Sam asked.

'There was no need. I know Edmond,' Leah said, ashamed to admit that there were times when she was afraid to question Edmond too closely about the business of the estate and about his nocturnal activities. He'd only spent a few nights at home during the preceding months.

Sam sighed heavily, put on his hat and went through the door. 'I'll try and find out what else is happening,' he said. 'One or two of the fellows may still be around.'

'You won't leave me and Mama Hannah alone here tonight will you, Sam?' She held out her hand to him but he did not take it.

'I'll be back soon,' Sam said. 'I can't understand why you sent word to the magistrates. I might still have persuaded Will and Sharper to relent. You could have given them their freedom. It's hard for me to believe we need to rely on settlers' help while our old friends are hiding from us in the bush.'

Leah felt a rush of anger at Sam. He knew, as well as she did, that she'd had little choice. The revolt had started at Roaring Creek and the owners of the mahogany camps up and down the creek were laying the blame at her door. They were afraid for their lives and for their losses in slaves and other property. There was no way she could avert worse disasters other than asking the magistrates to request the superintendent's help.

As she thought of these things, Leah watched Sam striding away from the house. He had broad shoulders and he swung his arms and flung his feet outwards as he walked. His walk reminded her, as it often did, of Graham Lawson, who had walked in just that way. She covered her face with her hands, not wanting to think about Graham Lawson, nor about the lives they'd once led in the slave yards at Eboe Town in Belize.

As she grew older her own features were growing to resemble his more and more. There were lines around her mouth and her hair had greyed at the temples, just as Graham Lawson's had done. It was not ever possible for her to forget that he had been her father. 'Am I like him inside as well?' she said out loud. 'Am I doing the same things he did or would have done? Is my heart hardening, drying out, like his did?'

Her lips were parched. She poured a glass of water from the clay jug on the table and drank thirstily. Drops of water trickled down her cheek and onto her neck. She felt feverish with anxiety. Hearing a sound from Hannah's room, Leah poured another glass of water and took it into her mother.

'Are we at the old place now?' Hannah asked. She looked eagerly around the room, and tried to rise from the rocking chair.

'We're going there, soon,' Leah said, 'as soon as Sam returns.' She said these words to her mother several times each day and sometimes at night when she awoke screaming that someone was beating her or trying to enter her room.

'Lawson's camp is better than here,' Hannah said. 'There are no high steps to climb there. I'll be able to come and go as I please. Take me there.'

Leah sat by her mother, soothing her, persuading her to take sips of water. Hannah had forgotten that Graham Lawson was dead, that Thomas McGilvrey had inherited his property and that, after McGilvrey's death, Leah had sold the Lawson logging concession to pay his British creditors.

As she rubbed Hannah's wrinkled hands and smoothed her hair, Leah thought of Will and Sharper. She guessed that they were probably hiding out in the caves at what had been Lawson's camp. She thought of the trees overshadowing the deep pool there, remembering the time, many years before, when Will and Sharper had narrowly escaped from the militia during another slave revolt. She hoped that they would get away, that they would make a run for the border. It would probably be their only chance.

Hannah fell into a deep sleep. She was snoring loudly as Leah tiptoed from the room. Outside the door, she paused for a

192

moment and put her hand against her heart which was beating too fast. Over the years, she'd learnt to solve many problems that had seemed insurmountable. Now, as she leaned against the wall of the house Thomas McGilvrey had built, she realized that she probably would never overcome her fear of living in the bush. When things were going well, when the logging camps were busy, the fire-hearth lit and the smell of stewed peccary, gibnut or mountain cow wafted across the compound, she had been able to forget her fears. Now, except for the natural sounds of the forest, everything was silent, at a standstill and the compound virtually deserted. She felt paralysed and uncertain which way to go. She was more afraid now than when Graham Lawson had first sent them upriver. For then there'd been her old friend, Will, whose protection she'd taken for granted. Will had revolted because she'd broken her promise to make and keep him as captain and main man on her estate.

Chapter 35

MAY 1820
WILL

Will inched his way cautiously along the branch of a giant fig tree with thick gnarled roots which had burrowed from the bank into the muddy depths of Roaring Creek. In his hand he held a long stick with a loop made of horse hair. Will whistled softly to an iguana which was mesmerized by the sound. He stretched the stick out and with a steady hand placed the loop around the iguana's neck and pulled the wriggling lizard into a canvas sack. As he climbed down the tree, he paused to look at the sunset through the enormous branches. Below him the water seemed to turn from a dark green to almost black as it flowed into the distance.

The voices of the black howler monkeys reverberated in the surrounding forest. The incessant noise reminded Will that Sharper had probably built the fire and was waiting for him to return with the iguana which they'd had a fancy to eat. When he rejoined Sharper in the camp, the fire had not been lit. Sharper stood staring down the path as though he'd seen something that frightened him.

'What is it?' Will asked, knotting the end of the sack and placing it on the ground.

'They know we are here,' Sharper said. 'I heard a sound and when I looked up there were two men looking at me from just over there.' He pointed to the narrow path through the bush. 'I fired a shot but there was no return. Do you suppose they were militia scouts?'

'I wouldn't be surprised,' Will said. 'Let's get a move on before they come back. It'll soon be night and we need to meet up with the others at the cave.' He slung the sack over his shoulder.

Sharper picked up their two guns and their powder flasks

and shot bags. He followed Will, who was moving quickly along the forest trail. 'We'd better speak quietly,' Sharper said. 'They may still be about.'

Will shrugged. He tried to keep his mind on the moments when he'd lingered in the fig tree overhanging the creek. As he'd watched the sunset and the shining water, a feeling of peace had crept over him and for a few minutes, the tension had left his body. It astonished him that, after all these years, he still did not have the freedom to build a little house somewhere deep in the forest by a creek or a river. It was what he'd always wanted. He had meant to have it. Why hadn't he made a run for it years ago? Bile rose in his throat and he spat on the dusty path. Behind him he heard Sharper's loud breathing. Will slowed his pace and looked around. Like himself, Sharper was drenched in sweat.

Will thought again of his imaginary house surrounded by a small plantation of vegetables, ground food and fruit trees. He saw himself sitting in a chair by his door in the cool of the evening smoking a pipe, smelling fish stew simmering on his own fire-hearth. He'd live alone in his hut far from human beings. 'I need somewhere safe and quiet,' he said to himself, 'that's what I want. I need a place of my own to build a new life.'

'It's not too late,' Sharper said. His voice was hopeful. 'I mean we can talk to the fellows, ask them to go back to work.'

'Roderick Horton killed Dover and three other fellows. We can't back down now.' Will said. He was thinking that perhaps he'd raise a hunting dog when he escaped from the settlement. 'Ah,' he thought to himself, 'perhaps I'll have a parrot too.' He would spend all his free evenings thinking of his youth in Africa and of his mother. Instead of forgetting his village, he found that he remembered the people there far more clearly than events that had happened only the year before.

'Leah must have sent to the superintendent for help,' Sharper said. 'They got here fast, didn't they?'

As he thought of Leah, Will felt a strange pain in his heart. 'I suppose she had to do it. The settlers won't rest until we are caught.'

'I warned the fellows about killing cattle and burning down so many houses,' Sharper said. 'She must be very frightened now.'

'Yes,' Will said. His throat tightened as he thought of Leah and her grown-up son, Edmond, who looked so much like her. His hair was soft and curly like his father's and he had the same dimple in his chin but other than that Will thought that Edmond's features were much like Leah's. In his dreams, Will had often pretended that Leah was his own sweetheart and that Edmond was his son.

When he'd first heard that McGilvrey had freed Leah and then married her shortly thereafter, he'd thought he would never recover from the shock and hurt. After several years had passed, Will began to understand and accept that obtaining freedom and security for herself and her family had always been the most important goals in Leah's life. He did not resent her choices for she had not encouraged his love for her in any way. He had kept his distance but remained loyal to Leah's interests.

Will had spent many good years as McGilvrey's main man on the estate. He and Edmond had been friends, or so he'd thought. He'd watched the boy grow up but he'd started to change after his father died. Under Roderick Horton's influence he'd started treating the slaves with such brutality that Will's authority was undermined. He felt himself caught between his fellow slaves and his loyalty to Leah.

However, when Leah had allowed Roderick Horton to remove him as captain and main man on her estate, his anger and resentment had overwhelmed the affection he'd always had for her. On Edmond's eighteenth birthday the year before, Leah had placed him in charge of the slaves and the entire estate. Will knew that Horton had watched him closely. He seemed to enjoy Will's humiliation before his fellow slaves.

'I'll do something,' Will said to Sharper one evening in early April. That afternoon they'd discovered a fresh stand of mahogany trees. Instead of rushing back with the news as they once would have done, Will and Sharper decided to spend the night in the forest.

'You always do,' Sharper said, handing Will his share of the salted pork and flour cakes which they carried in their bags. 'As far as I'm concerned, I've seen no mahogany trees.'

Only a few weeks before, if they'd stayed overnight in the bush, they'd have hunted for wild pig or gibnut to roast over an open fire but that evening they'd had no heart for a hunt.

'Just something in me, I guess,' Will said, replacing the food in Sharper's bag. 'I'm not hungry yet.'

'I'm glad it's there,' Sharper said. 'You should eat. Keep up your strength. We have to do something.'

'I'm not ever going back,' Will said, leaning against one of the mahogany trees. The tree was nearly one hundred feet high and about twelve feet across.

'I'm with you,' Sharper said. 'Mahogany trees don't spoil.' He passed the water bottle to Will. 'Some of the fellows are still with us.'

Will got to his feet. 'Let's go and see who's there.'

'I was thinking,' Sharper said. 'You are right. The way things are now, we can't ever go back. We'd be sold to other people, or worse.'

'We can try for the border,' Will said. 'It's dry weather.'

'I'm not as fast on my feet as I used to be – pain in my knees. I'll slow you down.'

'Pshaw,' Will said. 'Always talking about old age. We'll make it together. Let's go.'

The revolt had lasted unabated for several weeks until word reached Will and Sharper that the superintendent was on his way with the West India regiment to quell the uprising. Sharper's news about the militia spies disturbed Will greatly. He suspected that they had been betrayed by one of the slaves; this was not unusual in the life they led.

To lighten their load, Will freed the iguana and threw their food sacks into the bushes. Then they struck out for the secret trails to the caves by the pool. There they expected to find men gathered to continue their night journeys to the north. Will and Sharper walked in the shadows of the bushes and trees. The moon had risen. In its bright light everything stood out clearly.

If Leah had responded differently, Will thought to himself, he and Sukie could have made a kind of life for themselves on the far edges of the McGilvrey compound. He didn't love Sukie but she was a good woman and she cared for him. But in short order Leah had sold Sukie to Roderick Horton. Leah's actions puzzled Will. He had been loyal to her when he could have escaped a long time ago. After Thomas McGilvrey's death, it became clear to Will that Leah would always remain faithful to his memory. She continued to wear mourning black and worked as hard as anyone on the estate. She was that kind of person. Why had she denied him a hut for Sukie and himself, when he'd lost everything else?

'Why was she so angry with me?' Will asked Sharper when they'd left the compound before dawn the following day. Will and Sharper were walking to the rear of a gang of slaves heading for the forest.

'Jealous, I expect,' Sharper said, putting an arm around Will's shoulder. 'She and Sukie don't get on.'

'What more does she want? You'd think she'd be glad to get rid of Sukie.'

'She wouldn't want you and Sukie in a house together talking about her, planning to escape or burn the house down with her in it. That's how she's thinking.'

'Sukie's all right,' Will said.

'I didn't like the idea myself,' Sharper said.

'I'd lose you to Sukie.' He sniffed. 'She gets stranger to me every time I meet her.'

'How so?' Will asked.

'When I last saw her she kept talking about some Miskito king crowned in the new church in Belize.'

'George Frederick his name was. So Sukie told me anyway,' Will said, remembering how much Sukie had wanted to see the king. She believed he would have freed her from slavery.

'You didn't tell me about it,' Sharper said.

'It was a few years ago,' Will said.

He had hoped that Sharper and Sukie would become friends but that had not happened. He wondered what kind of life she would lead when Roderick Horton established his mahogany camp on the river. If his plans worked out, Will knew he would never see Sukie again.

It was almost daylight by the time they reached the edge of the forest near the pool and the caves. He and Sharper stopped to survey the broad expanse of water. Will was breathing fast as he peered through the leaves. There was no sign of life. The pool lay dark and still under the shadows of the surrounding trees.

Sharper whispered in his ear, 'There's nobody around. Let's turn back. They've already gone.'

Unable to believe his eyes, Will nodded. Slowly, they moved back from the bushes at the edges of the pool. They heard the snapping of twigs. Lifting their guns, they looked carefully around but the sound was not repeated.

Reassured, Will shrugged and made a sign to Sharper that they should make for the trail they'd just left. Overhead they heard the cry of an owl and the rustling of leaves. It was a fairly long walk to the trail and Will breathed a sigh of relief when he recognized the narrow footpath. As they emerged, a shot rang out. They tried to dash back the way they'd come but soldiers seemed to be everywhere shouting to each other.

Changing direction, Will and Sharper crashed through the bushes and thick vines on the opposite side. From the path behind them, a shot rang out and Sharper fell to the ground. Will fired back but his shots went wild. He bent down trying to drag Sharper into the bushes. He heard raised voices, the pounding of feet and then they were upon him. Will raised his gun again but, before he could fire, he felt a bullet hit his chest and he fell across the body of his friend, Sharper.

Epilogue

In the Name of God Almighty this eighth day of July in the year of our Lord one thousand eight hundred and twenty-two, I Leah Lawson McGilvrey of the settlement of Honduras, being at present of sound and perfect mind and memory but in a weak and infirm state of health, do deem it expedient to make this my last Will and Testament which is after the following manner.

First I desire that my body may be interred in a Christian-like manner and at a moderate expense which together with my just debts I desire may be paid as soon as possible after my decease. I desire that I be buried near to my mother Hannah O'Keefe and my husband Thomas McGilvrey at Roaring Creek.

Secondly, I will and bequeath unto Quasheba Neal, cook, and Berry Parker, assistant, the sum of ten pounds cash Jamaica currency to purchase mourning. My wearing apparel I leave to Quasheba Neal, a cow named Nelly and twenty-five pounds cash Jamaica currency. I leave to Berry Parker fifteen pounds cash Jamaica currency, my mahogany bed and a pit-pan.

Thirdly, I will and bequeath to my son, Edmond Thomas McGilvrey, at Glasgow, Scotland, the sum of two thousand pounds cash Jamaica currency and the silver and gold specie in the iron trunk which belonged to his father, Thomas McGilvrey.

Fourthly, I will and bequeath to my brother, Samuel Lawson, ten thousand acres of my concession at Roaring Creek, my house, also all my tools, cattle and two pit-pans. My brother, Samuel Lawson, was manumitted by me Christmas season, 1820.

Fifthly, I bequeath to my sister, Sukie Lawson Horton, fifty pounds cash Jamaica currency. Also my gold watch, silver thimbles, silver spoons and all crockery and glass.

Sixthly, I will and bequeath unto my people the remaining acres of my bank at Roaring Creek for their general benefit. Also it is my particular desire that the old women and the old men be allowed to retain their huts, their ground food plots and fruit from the trees on the estate for the remainder of their lives.

Seventhly, there is a balance due me by Roderick Horton on the purchase of the boy, Nathaniel, which should it not be paid before my death I desire it may be given up to him for the good of the child.

Eighthly, I desire that the whole of my slaves be set free from all manner of slavery and bondage.

Lastly I constitute and appoint Mr Alexander Muchelhany executor, Samuel Lawson executor and Sukie Lawson Horton executrix to this my last will and testament, hereby revoking and disenabling all former wills, legacies and bequests previous made, willed and bequeathed by me. In witness whereof I have hereunto set my signature, the day and the year as written above.

Leah Lawson McGilvrey
at Belize Town, Honduras

Signed published and
declared by the testatrix
to be her last will and testament
in the presence of Craig John Charles, Magistrate.

Glossary

apothecary	pharmacist or chemist
batteries	fortified emplacements for heavy guns
Baymen	the earliest white settlers of British Honduras, now Belize, which was also called the Bay Settlement or the Bay of Honduras before becoming a colony in 1865
bon	valid as security, a gift; in Belize, bon is pronounced bone
bram-bram	rowdy scene
brig	two-masted ship
bulwark	ship's side above deck
bump-and-bore	disorderly, noisy, confusing scene
calabash	shell or a gourd, used as a drinking vessel
case shot	bullets in an iron case that bursts open after firing
carronade	short, cast-iron cannon
cassava	edible root vegetable
cassia	tree bearing leaves from which senna is extracted; the cinnamon-like bark of this tree is used as spice
caye	small, low, offshore island consisting mostly of sand or coral islands (sometimes spelt cay or key)
coco-plum	small, round, brownish fruit with a single seed in a white, spongy, sharp-tasting pulp, borne on a shrub-like tree
coco-yam	round edible starchy tuber; the stem of this plant is a staple food in Belize
cohune nut	brown nut with a pointed tip, its tough fibre covering a black shell the size of a large egg; it is very hard and difficult to crack in order to get to the valuable, oil-yielding kernel
cohune palm	the nut comes in massive bunches on a palm tree of medium height

croton	any of various small tropical trees or shrubs with coloured, ornamental leaves
crow's nest	lookout platform or shelter, high on a ship's mast
doily	small ornamental mat made of lace placed on chair arms, headrests, etc.
dorey	small dug-out canoe used on rivers and along the coast
doubloon	gold coin formerly used in Spain and Spanish America
drogher	small vessel for transporting wood along the coast
gibnut	robust, brownish, coarse-haired rodent resembling an enlarged guinea-pig; this forest animal is much prized for its delicate meat
goombay or *gombay*	round or square-topped goat-skin drum played with the hands; several of them are used as central to the rhythm of a festive dance of the same name
guanacaste	large tree found on some Caribbean islands
guava cheese	confectionery made by boiling the pulp of ripe guavas with brown sugar and cutting into small blocks
gumbolimbo	tree which grows to about 24 metres in height; the bark is used as an antidote to poisonwood sap, insect bites, sunburn, rashes, skin sores, measles and other ailments
jalousie	blind or shutter having adjustable horizontal slats for regulating the passage of air and light
john crow bird	any large, black bird with a powerful beak
johnny cake or *journey cake*	kind of bread made from flour, milk or water, and shortening
lighter	flat barge, often with sails, to carry goods between a cargo ship and the shore
manumission	to set a slave free

mauger	thin, lean
Miskito Shore	(Mosquitia) region on the east coast of Nicaragua and Honduras, Central America; the name is derived from the Miskito, the original inhabitants
mountain cow	known in Belize as the mountain cow, the tapir is the largest of all land animals indigenous to Central America; it is a nocturnal, hoofed mammal with a short, flexible, protruding trunk; an adult weighs up to 650 pounds
negrito	the bark and root of the negrito tree yield a powerful astringent used for dysentery, diarrhoea, excessive menstruation, internal bleeding and other ailments
negro yam	large, long, edible starchy tuber
obeah	magic or voodoo whereby supernatural forces are used, often to evil ends
pappyshow	mock or ridicule
patakee	large, rectangular basket with bulging sides,lined with canvas as waterproofing; a covered type is used like a large knapsack by forest workers and fishermen
peccary	distant relative of the wild pig
pit-pan	square-ended, flat-bottomed boat that was the only river transport in the early days of the Belize settlement; pit-pans are hollowed out of a single log and can carry up to thirty people
pokonoboy	tall, slender many-stemmed palm with long, sharp black spines
real	silver coin formerly used in Spain and Latin America
sateen	cotton fabirc with a shiny finish
schooner	two-masted ship with the main mast taller than the front mast
scoggineal	cactus growing to 3 metres tall, with large thorny

	pads; a fresh pad is peeled, sliced and tied around the head to relieve headaches, fever, high blood pressure and other ailments
senna	laxative prepared from the dried leaves of a cassia tree
sheck'a or *shack'a*	rattle made by putting dried seeds in a coconut or other dried shell; the sheck'a is sometimes used as a musical instrument
sloop	small sailing vessel with a single mast
sorosi vine	growing to 1-2 metres in height; the leaves and vine are used as a household tonic to treat and prevent intestinal parasites, amoebas, anaemia, tiredness, painful periods, delayed menstruation, constipation, etc.
sour-sop	large, succulent fruit of an evergreen tree
tit-tie	common name in Belize for a variety of vines used as cord for tying and fastening
tommy-goff	venomous snake
yoke or *yoke-wood*	crossbar with two neckpieces to link a pair of oxen or other draft animals